RACIALISATION IN EARLY YEARS EDUCATION

This timely book explores the unique experiences of young black children during their first year of school and supports an understanding of how entry into the early years environment impacts on identity. Their stories emphasise the importance of listening to the voices of children themselves. A theoretical analysis of their first-hand experiences through a critical race lens illustrates how they are racialised through everyday interactions and routines. Chapters explore how personal and institutional attitudes might be reviewed to ensure that pedagogies and practices support the maintenance of black identities and challenge racism.

Enabling the reader to relate to the reality of black children's experience and offering valuable suggestions for effective anti-racist practice, chapters cover the following:

- the impacts of racism on black children's newly forming identities
- manifestations of racism in the early years sector
- multiculturalism and institutional whiteness
- effective communication with parents
- racialisation in relation to intersections of class, gender and race
- the role of playful pedagogies and friendships to support cultural identity.

This book enhances understanding of how race and racism operate across the early years sector and offers advice and reflective questions throughout. It is essential reading for students, practitioners and policymakers involved in early years provision.

Gina Houston has experience working with young black children and their families in England and Jamaica. Since qualifying as a teacher she has been a nursery school head teacher, trainer, early years advisor and children's centre manager. Working for a national charity, she has also supported practitioners in adopting anti-racist practice and policy across the early years sector.

Research Informed Professional Development for the Early Years

TACTYC (Association for Professional Development in Early Years)

The books in this series each focus on a different aspect of research in early childhood which has direct implications for practice and policy. They consider the main research findings which should influence practitioner thinking and reflection and help them to question their own practice alongside activities to deepen knowledge and extend understanding of the issues. Readers will benefit from clear analysis, critique and interpretation of the key factors surrounding the research as well as exemplifications and case studies to illustrate the research–practice or research–policy links. Supporting the development of critical reflection and up to date knowledge, the books will be a core resource for all those educating and training early years practitioners.

Exploring the Contexts for Early Learning
Challenging the School Readiness Agenda
Rory McDowall Clark

Building Knowledge in Early Childhood Education
Young Children are Researchers
Jane Murray

Early Childhood Education and Care for Sustainability
International Perspectives
Valerie Huggins and David Evans

Places for Two-Year-Olds in the Early Years
Supporting Learning and Development
Jan Georgeson and Verity Campbell-Barr

Racialisation in Early Years Education
Black Children's Stories from the Classroom
Gina Houston

RACIALISATION IN EARLY YEARS EDUCATION

Black Children's Stories from the Classroom

Gina Houston

Routledge
Taylor & Francis Group

LONDON AND NEW YORK

First published 2019
by Routledge
2 Park Square, Milton Park, Abingdon, Oxon OX14 4RN

and by Routledge
711 Third Avenue, New York, NY 10017

Routledge is an imprint of the Taylor & Francis Group, an informa business

British Library Cataloguing-in-Publication Data
A catalogue record for this book is available from the British Library

Library of Congress Cataloging-in-Publication Data
A catalog record for this book has been requested

ISBN: 978-1-138-15127-7 (hbk)
ISBN: 978-1-138-15287-8 (pbk)
ISBN: 978-1-315-10107-1 (ebk)

Typeset in Bembo
by Apex CoVantage, LLC

Printed and bound in Great Britain by
TJ International Ltd, Padstow, Cornwall

CONTENTS

ACKNOWLEDGEMENTS

Thanks to all those children, practitioners and parents who helped me to step out of my whiteness to understand that the Early Years sector is not as safe and value-free as it is often believed to be. Thanks to Professor Kevin Hylton, who showed me a new and more meaningful way to address racism in education through Critical Race Theory. Thanks to Sharon and Pat for their critical comments and encouragement. Last but definitely not least, thanks to Rory, who spent many hours editing and clarifying ideas in this book. Without you all these stories would not have been heard in the journey towards effective critical anti-racist practice in the early years.

SERIES EDITORS' PREFACE

Welcome to the fifth volume in the new, inspiring TACTYC book series. As part of the Association for Professional Development in the Early Years, TACTYC members believe that effective early years policies and practices should be informed by an understanding of the findings and implications of high-quality, robust research. TACTYC focuses on developing the knowledge base of all those concerned with early years education and care by creating, reviewing and disseminating research findings and by encouraging critical and constructive discussion to foster reflective attitudes in practitioners. Such a need has been evident in the resounding success of events such as our conferences, where speakers make clear connections between research and practice for delegates. Early years practitioners and those who support their professional development engage enthusiastically with early childhood research and understand how it is likely to impact upon, and enhance, practice. They acknowledge that research has a distinct role to play in effective work in early years education and care, and that they should be part of a 'research–rich education system'.

TACTYC is an organisation with a specific focus on the professional development of all those involved in early childhood with the express purpose of improving practices to enhance the well-being of young children. Its reputation for quality research and writing includes its international *Early Years* journal. This book series is likely to be popular with those who value the journal as it will add to its range and scope. Our aim for the series is to help those who educate and train early years practitioners at all levels to understand the implications and practical interpretation of recent research, and to offer a rationale for improving the quality and reach of practice in early years education and care.

It is not always easy for busy trainers and practitioners to access contemporary research and translate it into informed and reflective practice. These books are intended to promote the benefits of applying research in an informed way to develop quality pedagogical practices. Each individual book in this series will explore a range of different topics within a theme. This fifth book considers the issues involved in **children's experiences of racialisation in early years education**. Writing from a critical race theory perspective, it discusses the implications of Gina's research about how children come to understand how they, and others, are positioned according to their racial identity. Critical Race Theory takes as a starting point a 'fundamental truth that racism is embedded in society and its institutions' (Chapter 1, p. 14). The research, based on observation and one-to-one discussions, therefore foregrounds the voices of seven 4-year-old children with African-Caribbean heritage as they enter reception classes. Four boys and three girls share their thoughts and feelings about the situations they face in daily life in four schools. From her analysis, Gina draws out suggested questions and prompts to support practitioners in reflective practice. This exciting book challenges us to see these young children's everyday experiences through the lens of racialisation. It extends the opportunity to think about how adult pedagogic choices can inadvertently marginalise or connect to home life and young children's identities. The theory and research findings are presented in a clear, unambiguous way, while acknowledging the often complex relationships between what we know and what is possible in practice.

Interest in this phase of education and care has been growing exponentially in the last few years, and there is now a rich source of early years research on which writers may draw. The claim is frequently made that policies are 'evidence-based', but this is not the same as rigorous, impartial research. Many policy and practice documents purport to be based on 'evidence', but this depends to a large extent on the political framework and ideology in place at different periods in time – few governments have the scope in their relatively short elected periods to give strategic consideration to the complex implications of different research outcomes for policies and practice. What is politically and economically expedient at the time is too often the driving force behind decisions about young children and their families.

All the writers in this series have been asked to present their particular focus and to outline the issues and challenges within that framework, which are relevant for early years practitioners. Exploring aspects of early years practice, based on research and sound theoretical underpinning, the writers will offer guidance on how findings can be analysed and interpreted to inform the continuing process of developing high-quality early years practice. They will examine the research background to each topic and offer considered views on why the situation is as it is, and how it might move forward within the frameworks of imposed curricula and assessments. They will offer thoughtful advice to practitioners for dealing with the challenges faced within that particular focus and will suggest relevant follow-up reading and web-based materials to support further reflection, practice and curriculum implementation. Each book will also identify where further research is needed and will help tutors, trainers and practitioners to understand how they can contribute to research in this field.

Early years education and care is universally contentious, especially in relation to how far those outside the field, e.g. politicians and policymakers, should intervene in deciding what constitutes successful early years pedagogy, curriculum and assessment. The main focus of the series will be on practice, policy and provision in the UK, but writers will also draw on international research perspectives, as there is a great deal to learn from colleagues in other national contexts.

The series particularly targets readers qualified at Level 6, or students on such courses, who are preparing for roles in which they will be expected to educate and train other practitioners in effective early years practices. There will be many others who will find the books invaluable: leaders of early years settings, who often have an education, training and professional development role in relation to their staff (and may well be qualified at Level 6 or beyond), will similarly find the series useful in their work. Academics and new researchers who support the training and development of graduate leaders in early years will also appreciate the books in this series. Readers will benefit from clear analysis, critique and interpretation of the key factors surrounding the research as well as exemplifications and case studies to illustrate the links between research and policy as well as research and practice. The books will support the development of critical reflection and up-to-date knowledge, and will be a core resource for all those educating and training early years practitioners.

In summary, research-based early years practice is a relatively new field, as much of practitioners' work with young children over recent years has been based on the implementation of policy documents, which are often not grounded in rigorous, clear, unambiguous research evidence. The main aim of the TACTYC series is to help tutors and trainers to enable practitioners to become more informed advocates for provision of high-quality services for children and their families. This will be achieved by promoting the benefits of applying research in an informed way to develop the quality of practice.

Professor Emerita Janet Moyles and Professor Jane Payler

INTRODUCTION

Young children do not often get an opportunity in the busy world of the class-room to voice their personal perspectives on their early experiences as they become independent in the new world of school. This book attempts to give seven black children that opportunity. Their stories indicate how everyday interactions in their reception classrooms impact on their early education, offering an insight into how black children interact with the new white middle-class culture of the school to maintain their black, British identities. Although these particular children are in reception classes, their experiences can be related to settings across the early years sector to support an inclusive agenda that addresses the racialisation of children. Throughout my long career in early years education I have taken the position that race and racism is a reality for young children in the Early Years Foundation Stage (EYFS). I have heard, like many others, numerous comments made by black children such as those below that reveal how racism is ever-present in their lives:

- a boy aged 2 chanting the phrase 'blackie, blackie, blackie' because this is what he is called in the nursery
- a boy aged 3 constantly 'washing the black' from his hands
- a girl aged 4 asking, 'Why do all the black people have rubbish jobs?'
- a boy aged 5 being told by a black peer with a lighter skin tone, 'I'm glad I'm not black like you'.

The effects of racism are still as apparent today as they were when I began my teaching career 40 years ago. My 5-year-old, black mixed-race grandson attends a predominantly white school. He was worried about going on holiday to Jamaica. He explained his concern as being 'because the sun may make my skin darker and then my friends at school won't like me anymore'. Fanon describes the range of emotions children feel as they learn how some in society view their identities first as black, and then as subject to the stereotypes this infers. He tells how he is 'angered', 'tormented', 'pursued' and 'disturbed' by the 'false stereotypes and the singular identity of blackness' (2008, p. 88).

The above comments contradict a view that young children are not aware of race and naively repeat racist comments (Hart, 2009). They are indicators of the ever-present effects of racism both in and out of school on young black children's identity and education. These experiences are supported by the statement that

> racism surrounds us, permeates our ideas and conversations, focuses our relationships with one another, shapes our practices, and drives much in our personal, social and political lives. There are few social forces so strong. Children are neither immune to it nor unaware of its power. A social reality this mighty is bound to become an integral part of their lives, and thus it endures from generation to generation, perhaps changing somewhat in form but still strong in its impact. . . . Racism intersects with their lives in a flood of elaborate, blatant and subtle ways – from the definition of identity and self, to the performance of hurtful practices, to various articulations of dominant group power.
>
> *(Van Ausdale and Feagin, 2001, p. 198)*

This statement is even more relevant following the increase in overt racist incidents since the 2016 referendum result for Britain to leave the European Union. The open border policy has resulted in blame for declining public services, unemployment and worsening social conditions being placed by some on immigrants from Europe. The recent racist attacks on Eastern Europeans coincide with the rise of Islamophobia, placing responsibility on all Muslims for the terrorist activities of an extreme few. Children are not immune from racism in society and are inevitably influenced by actions and opinions of their elders. Although the reality of racism has underpinned my commitment to anti-racism, I understand that my privileged position as a white middle-class educator can influence my perspectives on racism and the way it operates at all levels to permeate the lives of young black children. For this reason I embarked on a doctoral research study to prioritise their voices to hear their own realities of how being black impacts on their early years education. This book attempts to represent their experiences and initiate discussion towards provision of an early years environment that can better support.

The research project

Listening to the voices of young children through observation has been an integral part of early years research (Murray, 2018). However, the voices of young black children in schools have often been excluded as a research focus. Research on black pupils in England has predominantly been on attainment and disaffection in older black boys in particular (Mac An Ghail, 1994; Sewell, 1996; Byfield, 2008; Gillborn, 2016). Other studies such as those of Mirza (2009) and Rollock (2012) have discussed how the intersections of race and gender impact on the education of black British girls in the secondary phase. The intersections of race and class on the education of black pupils are the research focus for Rollock et al. (2015). They discuss how class impacts on black pupils in primary and secondary education through interviews with black parents. Research evidence has indicated that racism in education at both institutional and personal levels affect pupils' dispositions to learning, resulting in disproportionate numbers of black boys being excluded from school.

Young children have sometimes been missing from research through constructions of childhood that propose a cognitive immaturity that prevents an understanding of abstractions such as racialisation processes. They are often believed to be too young to have valid opinions and are viewed as 'vulnerable recipients of interventions' rather than 'social actors and agents' who can contribute to the research process (Smith, 2013, p. 3). The lack of research on black children's early experiences in school has resulted in misunderstandings of how racism impacts on young children's education, as many previous studies have produced data from attitudinal tests such as those by Milner (1975) discussed in Chapter 3. These methods can result in researcher-led interpretations rather than a child's reflections on their racialising experiences. The methods applied to this project are in recognition of the need to understand how being black can influence children's education when entering mainstream school. Ladson-Billings and Tate IV (2009, p. 174) propose that for a complete analysis of the education system and to say 'anything useful' about education it is essential to include the voices of 'people of color' in educational research. A predominance of the voices of young white children and omission of discussion on race in early years research has marginalised an analysis of black children's experiences in English schools. Connolly (1998, p. 5) emphasises the importance of a focus on research with young children centring on the 'subjective world of the children themselves' rather than on predetermined objectives of the researcher. He adopts participatory methods to share the voices of the children to understand how the intersections of race and gender impact on their experiences in school. Data from interviews and naturalistic observations indicate the active role they play in 'managing, adapting and reproducing discourses on race' and gender in their social worlds. This study centres on the experiences of seven black children as they enter reception classes at the age of 4 years. Four boys and three girls with African-Caribbean heritage took part in the study. The emphasis throughout is on the importance of privileging young black children's voices as a means by which social realities of race and intersections with gender and class can be understood by the researcher from within rather than as an onlooker into the black child's experiences in early years education.

Schools were chosen for research sites so as to reduce the many variables that could impact on both data collection and interpretations. Other early years settings vary more than schools regarding management and staffing; ages of children attending; funding and resourcing; hours; and days of attendance. However, the issues arising from the research are common to black children who attend any early years setting and are important considerations for all those responsible for the care and education of young children across both the maintained and non-maintained sectors. The four schools participating in the research are all in an inner-city borough in England with a large African-Caribbean community; African-Caribbeans have been settling in the UK since post-war immigration from Commonwealth countries in the Caribbean. There is a general commitment in the local authority to support the education of black children and an acknowledgement at all levels of management regarding the impact of racism in education. The ethnically diverse population lives in both privately owned and rented accommodation in the borough. Some council housing remains in modernised estates with social housing provided through partnerships between housing associations and the local authority. These are alongside highly priced privately owned properties in neighbouring residential streets. There is a mixed community in relation to class, partly due to the proximity of the borough to employment in the centre of the city and good transport links attracting private home ownership. The schools are within an approximate 5-mile radius of each other and, although they are situated in similarly diverse communities, have very different school populations in relation to race and ethnicity. A transient population results in fluctuating pupil demographics throughout the school year. All children, schools and staff are given pseudonyms in the book to protect their anonymity. The children were offered the opportunity to choose their own research names as it was explained that their true identity would not be known. To further protect their anonymity it is not necessary to know details of the children themselves or their schools as the issues arising from their stories are not unique and can be applied to many black children of their age in any early years setting.

Hearing the children's voices through narrative

The children's voices are heard through data from both participatory and non-participatory methods of observation and informal discussions during daily routines. These methods aim to promote an understanding of the children's experiences through their many idiosyncratic forms of representation (Malaguzzi, 1993). Forms of representation such as language, play activity, behaviour, facial and bodily expressions, and creativity give opportunities for children to be active participants in the project. Naturalistic observation and one-to-one discussions with children took place to hear their views and to facilitate reflection and interpretation from their own positions. Observation followed by in-depth conversations can also counter racialised stereotypes and give alternative perspectives on children's experiences towards a more critical interpretation of their actions through a 'third ear' (Foreman and Fye, 1998, p. 249). This approach can decentre meaning from an adult perspective, challenging preconceived stereotypes. Chesworth (2015) emphasises the importance of a focus on research with young children centring on the subjective world of the children themselves rather than on predetermined objectives of the researcher. When young black children's stories are heard, they can be a pertinent means by which to understand how they interpret their experiences of racialisation. Their stories told in this book tell how they use agency and cultural wealth to oppose challenges to their black identities and experiences from home. The use of counter-narratives in Chapters 3, 4 and 5 of this book places the children's experiences in everyday situations, giving the reader opportunities to relate to the reality of black children's life in the classroom. Analysis of their stories allows for a theoretical understanding of how they are racialised through their everyday interactions as they participate in classroom routines. The stories are told in the form of composite narratives to apply and consolidate data from across the research period around emergent themes. The narratives differ in the way they are composed to focus on the specific issues raised for each of the children as indicated at the beginning of the relevant chapters. These methods are discussed further in Chapter 1 as frequently used in Critical Race Theory (CRT) to provide stories of othered communities, to counter common perspectives from the white population. Interpretations of the narratives will vary depending on readers. Those in this book are through the eye of a white researcher and are aimed at an understanding of how racism impacts on black children's experiences in their early days at school. Readers who experience racism first-hand may interpret the stories differently from a position of racial realism. It is important to discuss the counter-narratives with others to hear the diverse interpretations and perspectives with the common aim to take united action against racism in early years education.

Terminology explained

Some terms used in this book in both early years and race relations discourses are defined here, as they are open to multiple interpretations. Osgood et al. (2016) outline the qualifications available for career progression in the early years sector. The report describes the ad hoc approach to the development of an early years qualification that results in some confusion regarding the different terms for qualifications across levels and access to quality of training opportunities. There are disparities in pay, conditions and responsibilities for staff in the early years sector despite the common professional commitment to the care and education of young children. Until clarity is confirmed in this respect, the term practitioner is used in this book to recognise the generic role of all those working with children in the early years. 'Teacher' is assigned only to those who have ultimate classroom responsibility when it is textually relevant to denote the levels of responsibility designated in schools. It is not intended to discriminate between members of the team in terms of status. Through a fundamental principle within the early years sector, teams work together to jointly educate and care for children.

Other terminology has various interpretations in both academic and in social contexts. The term black is applied here to denote the 'important social, historical, cultural and economic experiences of those who would identify their family origins in the Caribbean' (Gillborn, 2008, p. 2). Black also distinguishes between Caribbean communities with African-Caribbean heritage from those with ascendance from the Asian, European, South American or Middle Eastern diaspora who have a history of settlement in the Greater and Lesser Antilles from early colonisation to the present day. This definition recognises the different experiences of race and racism in Britain within communities and can avoid reified interpretations of diversity across cultural heritages. There is a danger of stereotyping communities through an interpretation of black referring to a common socio-cultural identity. When using the term here, a fundamental premise is the unique cultural diversity and racialising experiences of black British, African-Caribbean communities.

Race is interpreted in this book as a means of identification for those living in racialised societies such as Britain as well as 'a social construct of resistance' against inequalities (Darder and Torres, 2009, p. 157). The term is used from an anti-essentialist perspective as a social phenomenon with no permanent or agreed definition, which recognises that meaning can change according to the political, economic and social conditions impacting on society at any one time (Hylton, 2009). This is in contrast to a deterministic, biological definition of race that relies on visible characteristics alone, such as physical features. Inverted commas are not used in this book when referring to race to denote the separation of the ideological non-essentialised meaning from the scientific meaning. The term is placed in inverted commas only when it specifically refers to a biological definition. Terms for other socially constructed relations such as gender are not marked in the same way, suggesting the use of scare quotes serves to marginalise race within a discourse of inequalities. Because some terms such as gender are not in inverted commas, it does not mean that they are interpreted as biologically determined, and so this should be the case for all socially constructed terms (Preston, 2009). By not using parentheses, race is acknowledged as a socially constructed interpretation alongside all other areas of inequality intersecting with black children's racialising experiences.

The term racisms includes all othered groups in society who are exposed to racism through social constructions such as those of race and religion. Definitions within the concept of racisms can change due to social, political and economic circumstances. Examples of racisms in Britain are evident in the increasing racist attacks against Jews and Muslims since the rise in Europe of right-wing political parties partly as a response to immigration issues and international terrorist incidents. Current economic conditions have given rise to othered white communities such as those from Eastern Europe being victimised since the decision to leave the European Union and restrict immigration to Britain. Although the racialising experiences of othered white ethnic groups are included in the definition of racisms, their whiteness gives them opportunities to assume a public identity that enables generational assimilation into white British society. By masking their identities they can choose to become invisible in society through a perceived identity of whiteness, thus creating some protection from racism (Leonardo, 2009a). Despite the fluid interpretation of racisms and the impact on all those who are othered in the hierarchy of a white British identity, racialised identities remain a constant reality for those who are marginalised through their physical appearance.

Robinson and Diaz define the other as 'those groups that have been marginalised, silenced, denigrated or violated, in opposition to the privileged and powerful groups that are identified as representing the idealised, mythical norm in society' (2006, p. 24). This book focuses on the consequences of the historical and consistent racialising factors and unique experiences of black British children in context with other racialised groups during current social relations in Britain.

Reflections on whiteness in the research process

Although whiteness will be discussed further in Chapter 1 as an important element of Critical Race Theory (CRT), a discussion of the term is included in the introduction to this book, as it influences how the research data is collected, interpreted and analysed through the children's stories. This is particularly relevant to this research as the researcher is white and is gathering data from black participants, posing ethical questions. Constantine-Simms (1995) sees it as problematic for a white researcher to research the black experience as endemic racism in society can impact on white truth, making it impossible for value-free research and academic objectivity. A CRT theoretical framework for the research enables engagement in the research process through historical and political awareness of whiteness as a dominant ideology in British society. Acceptance of hierarchical relationships based on whiteness allows for an interpretation of the black experience facilitated through a lens that acknowledges the inevitable effects of racism and the processes in education that contribute to the racialisation of children. This positioning can support white researchers to discount preconceived ideas of black children's early experiences formed through centring their own personal attitudes and preformed ideas in interpretation of data.

As well as the social positioning of the researcher in relation to the data, emotional dynamics and language must be taken into account in the racialised relationships between the researcher and participants (Gunaratnam, 2003). Connolly's (2008) research indicates how children are aware of the intersections of race and gender when interacting with adults. Responses to him as a white male researcher impact on his interpretation of data as being true and genuine representations of the children's social worlds. He concludes that although race and gender influence children's interactions with adults, they should be understood with the recognition that there are multiple voices depending on the context in which they are heard and that all have validity if interpreted reflectively. Recognition of children's agency in determining how intersections of race and gender form their experiences was a constant consideration throughout this research. By focusing on the CRT precept of social justice it is possible to challenge a personal embodiment of whiteness and influence the research process through reflexive engagement with the processes of whiteness (Preston, 2013, p. 3). This can be supported through a CRT methodology that is conscious of the endemic existence of racism in society alongside a commitment to racial justice that better allows for interpretations of black children's experiences. To do this there must be an acknowledgement of whiteness and consequential privileges on racialised dynamics and interpretation of data. For this study it was necessary to break down hierarchical relationships between the white adult researcher and child participants, parents and practitioners. Time was spent in the classroom taking part in daily routines and interacting with participants informally before the beginning of the research period. This gave the researcher and participants opportunities to challenge any preconceived ideas regarding both the research project and the inevitable barriers in relationships due to existing hierarchies such as status, age, gender and race.

Leonardo (2009b) suggests that the experiences of racism, from the standpoint of racial realism and the visibility of being black, mean there is an inevitability of a racialised identity that impacts differently on those being researched compared to that of the white researcher. This creates a concern regarding white academics that 'work on race' as they cannot position themselves through experiences of racism, as do those they study (Preston, 2013, p. 3). Questioning of cross-cultural research can be interpreted as an important element of academic discourse, encouraging greater reflexivity in search of an understanding that constantly changes in context with differing perspectives (Banks, 2001). A white researcher inevitably has what Bradbury (2013, p. 46) terms as a 'constituted subjectivity' impacting on data collection and interpretation. This can be problematic, although it is not an inevitable barrier to understanding realities for black children. It is possible to challenge this subjectivity through recognition of how an invisibility of whiteness and acceptance of white norms as truth in early years education contributes to the racialisation of black children. Interpretation of research data always has an element of subjectivity that can be questioned and discussed towards a clearer understanding of black children's experiences as they begin school. What is evident in the children's stories is how resilient and competent they are as they uncompromisingly assert their black identities in the domination of whiteness within the school culture.

The chapters

The focus for this book is children's stories that tell of their unique experiences during their first year in school. The reception class year provides a foundation for future learning and is important when forming dispositions to education and the learning environment. Some chapters tell directly of their daily activity through their stories while other chapters give a theoretical and contextual background to interpretations of their experiences. Each chapter gives suggestions for reflective practice to help trainers and practitioners consider their own beliefs and values and how these may impact on practice. Although this may be a challenging experience, it can be achieved through ongoing dialogue within staff teams necessary to support black children at the beginning of their early years education.

Chapter 1 introduces Critical Race Theory (CRT) as a theoretical lens to understand the particular issues for black children as they adapt to an environment dominated by a culture which in many ways differs from that in their homes and communities. Central tenets of CRT are outlined to frame interpretations of the stories that tell how black children may be racialised through institutional procedures and practices. By centralising the realities of race and racism in black children's lives it is possible to understand how whiteness impacts on everyday interactions to racialise them as the other. Whiteness is defined in the chapter as a social construct, which once recognised can be addressed to provide more inclusive learning environments for all children. Hearing counter-narratives of othered communities towards effective action against racism in education provides the rationale for the children's stories. CRT supports this process by centring race in interpretation of their experiences to challenge the environmental and interactional processes that discriminate and racialise.

Chapter 2 explores how children are racialised through concepts applied in CRT that impact on newly forming identities as they make relationships with peers and adults in the classroom. The effects of racial micro-aggressions on black children's relationships when adapting to new cultural norms is discussed in relation to how this impacts on their identities. It is suggested that conflicts they meet in the classroom through expectations of whiteness may have a psychological effect through double-consciousness or a proxy identity in school. By recognising challenges black children may have in the new school environment, colour-blind indifference can be addressed and more equitable learning environments can result that support their identities and experiences from home.

The following three chapters begin with counter-narratives composed of seven children's experiences. Each story is analysed from a starting point of a common theme emerging from the data that applies to all the children in the study at perhaps different levels of significance. Children's voices are heard through a CRT lens as a theoretical frame to understand their unique experiences when entering a social environment that brings new challenges. Analyses of their stories are not absolute, as readers will place their own interpretations on the children's experiences. However, they are intended to raise discussion through acknowledgement of the effects of race and racism on young black children and how they challenge their racialisation to adapt to the norms of the school. The stories indicate the value of a critical pedagogy that allows time for listening to children to understand their nuanced experiences that may otherwise remain unrealised or considered insignificant. All three stories relate experiences that racialise black children, highlighting the need for critical interventions. At the end of each of the three chapters suggestions are made for reflection on practice to address systemic and interactional processes that contribute to their racialisation. These are intended as a starting point for ongoing questioning and action to provide safe spaces for black children where they are supported to challenge racialising experiences and affirm positive learner identities.

Devon's story (Chapter 3) tells of his activity in the school forest area, showing the importance of playful pedagogy that allows black children to maintain identities formed in the home whilst accommodating to the new cultural norms of the reception class. Extended opportunity for role play enables him to express his identity through his friendships with two boys. Alan, his white 'special friend' gives him support for adapting to the norms of whiteness as he feels his black identity is accepted as a positive aspect of the close relationship. When Devon needs to reassert his blackness he turns to Neil, his black friend, for support. His story indicates how black children are aware of processes that racialise their identities and how they use their agency to address marginalisation. Devon's story also raises issues of how intersections of race and gender can stereotype early learner identities and impact on their future education.

Kylie's and Sonic's narrative (Chapter 4) tells of how two black children manage a pedagogy that allows limited opportunities for exploring concepts through play. The roles of multiculturalism and institutional whiteness are suggested as major factors in the early processes of othering black children in the early years of education which can further impact future experiences in school. Sonic's and Kylie's story illustrates how they develop personal learner identities to gain access to opportunities for learning. Parental views on early years pedagogy are discussed as important, as they can be contradictory to those of practitioners. It is important to establish strategies for communication with parents to build meaningful professional relationships. A broad perspective on black pupils' experiences through listening to counter-stories can support understanding of parental perspectives and concerns for their children's education.

Pina's experiences of racialisation (Chapter 5) come from actions in the classroom and remarks at playtime about her hair used to exclude her and dominate the resources. They show how young children may have already internalised hierarchies of physical characteristics, with whiteness being accepted as the most desirable. Pina cuts her hair to express the effects of racial micro-aggressions experienced not only through verbal insults but also through images portrayed in and out of school as the norm of physical desirability. Her counter-narrative shows how racialised attitudes of some adults and children to physical characteristics of appearance, in this case black children's hair texture and styling, can affect peer group relationships and contribute to their racialisation. Both intentional and unintentional racial micro-aggressions impact on the children's daily classroom interactions and contribute to newly forming racialised identities as children adapt to the whiteness of the school environment. This includes the particular issue of racialisation through hierarchies of beauty, as evidenced through the majority of children in the study who were made conscious of their hair in interactions with both children and adults. It is important to acknowledge the social context of the racialisation process in relation to intersections of class, gender and race to understand the impact on children's education. Racialised and gendered hierarchies reproduced in the classroom can lead to invisibility of the predominant culture of whiteness and a lack of understanding regarding the black experience in education. This chapter emphasises the importance of a critical, reflexive pedagogy to challenge racial micro-aggressions and racialised hierarchies.

Chapter 6 places an alternative perspective on the event of Pina cutting her hair. Dawn's story tells of how a white teacher in a multiracial reception class manages her commitment to provide equality for all children in a safe learning environment. The composite narrative is derived from data across the four schools and includes the concerns of many white practitioners involved in the research. Three main issues are highlighted through Dawn's story. The first is the impact of race and racism on black children's newly forming identities as they begin their school careers. This includes how whiteness can marginalise and exclude children with othered identities. Colour-blind approaches can deny the effects of being black in a racially hierarchal society, leaving black children unsupported. Dawn's story indicates the need for policy formation through a consensus in meanings and understandings of race and racism to develop strategies that challenge racialisation processes in both personal and institutional practices. The third issue concerns the value of a critical, reflexive pedagogy that enables and recognises children's socio-cultural experiences and knowledge. Reflective practice allows for practitioners to discuss and examine their own attitudes and privileges of whiteness to recognise the impact of societal values on all children.

Chapter 7 discusses how the value of playful pedagogies contrasts with current demands of curriculum delivery and accountability that prevent equality of access to early years education for black children. The current managerial culture of the classroom with priority on assessment of development levels leaves few opportunities to observe or interact with children during their self-directed play. Classrooms promoting playful pedagogies, such as those contextualising the stories of Devon and Pina, can offer extended opportunities for children to frame their learning through cultural knowledge from the home. It is through extended periods of self-directed activity that they can build on previous experiences to learn and understand during explorations in the school environment. A structured, overmanaged pedagogy denies these crucial foundations through which children learn, speak and imagine (Giroux, 2009). Multicultural education is often viewed as an appropriate way to provide for the diverse cultures of young children. The second part of this chapter argues that without a critical frame that recognises the processes and procedures that deny cultural representation and do not challenge all levels of racism, multiculturalism can marginalise rather than include black children. By isolating children's cultural heritages through celebrations and special events they can feel excluded from the mainstream curriculum by home cultures being viewed as exotic and outside British mainstream culture.

The final chapter in the book takes ideas emerging from the children's experiences and suggests ways in which practitioners can address issues of racialisation individually or/and with colleagues. It is not the intention of this chapter to give practical suggestions as this approach may be interpreted through a non-critical multicultural curriculum. The aim of the chapter is to raise issues for consideration and discussion that can support inclusion of British children's diverse identities across all aspects of procedures and practices in all early years settings. To meet the aims of practitioners to establish and maintain environments that provide for the education of all young children, it is the responsibility of everyone to challenge racialising processes alongside their own personal attitudes and what are often unconscious biases. For this it is necessary to discuss how changes can be made at micro and macro levels within an ethos that makes it acceptable to raise issues of race. Lane (2008) refers to this ethos as a no-blame culture that allows for freedom of opinion where personal and professional views can be openly and honestly raised and discussed and good practice shared. The children's stories in this book can contribute to supporting discussions towards understanding how race and racism operate across early years sectors to racialise children and how this can be challenged to provide more inclusive early years education.

References

Banks, J. A. (2001) *Cultural Diversity and Education.* Boston, USA: Allyn and Bacon.

Bradbury, A. (2013) *Understanding Early Years Inequality: Policy, Assessment and Young Children's Identities.* Oxon: Routledge.

Byfield, C. (2008) *Black Boys Can Make It.* Staffordshire: Trentham Books.

Chesworth, L. (2015) A Deeper Understanding of Play, in Brock, A. (ed.), *The Early Years Reflective Practice Handbook.* Oxon: David Fulton.

Connolly, P. (1998) *Racism, Gender Identities and Young Children.* London: Routledge.

Connolly, P. (2008) Race, Gender and Critical Reflexivity in Research with Young Children, in Christensen, P. and James, A. (eds.), *Research with Children, Perspectives and Practices,* 2nd ed. Oxon: Routledge.

Constantine-Simms, D. (1995) The Role of the Black Researcher in Educational Research, in Showunmi, V. (ed.), *Teachers for the Future.* Staffordshire: Trentham Books.

Darder, A. and Torres, R. (2009) After Race: An Introduction, in Darder, A., Baltodano, M. and Torres, R. (eds.), *The Critical Pedagogy Reader,* 2nd ed. Oxon: Routledge.

Fanon, F. (2008) *Black Skins, White Masks.* London: Pluto Press.

Foreman, G. and Fye, B. (1998) Negotiated Learning, in Foreman, G. and Fye, B. (eds.), *The Hundred Languages of Children and the Reggio Approach: Advanced Reflections,* 2nd ed. London: Ablex Publishing.

Gillborn, D. (2008) *Racism in Education, Coincidence or Conspiracy.* Oxon: Routledge.

Gillborn, D. (2016) White Lies: Things That Were Told about Race and Education That Weren't True. Available from www.birmingham.ac.uk/schools/education/research/2016/gillborn. Accessed 10 January 2017.

Giroux, H. A. (2009) Teacher Education and Democratic Schooling, in Darder, A., Baltodano, M. and Torres, R. (eds.), *The Critical Pedagogy Reader.* Oxon: Routledge.

Gunaratnam, Y. (2003) *Researching 'Race' and Ethnicity.* London: Sage Publications.

Hart, I. (2009) *The Myth of Racist Kids.* London: Manifesto Club.

Hylton, K. (2009) *'Race' and Sport, Critical Race Theory.* Oxon: Routledge.

Ladson-Billings, G. and Tate IV, W. F. (2009) Toward a Critical Race Theory of Education, in Darder, A., Baltodano, M. and Torres, R. (eds.), *The Critical Pedagogy Reader,* 2nd ed. Oxon: Routledge.

Lane, J. (2008) *Young Children and Racial Justice.* London: National Children's Bureau.

Leonardo, Z. (2009a) *Race, Whiteness and Education.* Oxon: Routledge.

Leonardo, Z. (2009b) The Color of Supremacy, in Taylor, E., Gillborn, D. and Ladson-Billings, G. (eds.), *Foundations of Critical Race Theory in Education.* Oxon: Routledge.

Mac An Ghail, M. (1994) *Making of Men: Masculinities, Sexualities and Schooling.* Berkshire: Open University Press.

Malaguzzi, L. (translated by Gandini, L.) (1993) For an Education Based on Relationships, in *Young Children,* 49 (1) pp. 1–12. National Association for the Education of Young Children. Available from www.reggioalliance.org/downloads. Accessed 13 June 2014.

Milner, D. (1975) *Children and Race*. London: Penguin.

Mirza, H. S. (2009) *Race, Gender and Educational Desire: Why Black Women Succeed and Fail*. Oxon: Routledge.

Murray, J. (2018) *Building Knowledge in Early Childhood Education*. Oxon: Routledge.

Osgood, J., et al. (2016) Early Years Training and Qualifications Study. Available from http/tactic.org.uk/research

Preston, J. (2009) *Whiteness and Class in Education*. London: Springer.

Preston, J. (2013) *Whiteness in Academia: Counter-Stories of Betrayal and Resistance*. Newcastle upon Tyne: Cambridge Scholars Publishing.

Robinson, K. and Jones Diaz, C. (2006) *Diversity and Difference in Early Childhood Education*. Berkshire: Open University Press.

Rollock, N. (2012) The Invisibility of Race: Intersectional Reflections on the Liminal Space of Alterity, in *Race, Ethnicity and Education*, 15 (1) pp. 65–82.

Rollock, N., et al. (2015) *The Colour of Class*. Oxon: Routledge.

Sewell, T. (1996) *Black Masculinities and Schooling: How Black Boys Survive Modern Schooling*. Staffordshire: Trentham Books.

Smith, A. (2013) Children's Rights and Early Childhood Education. Available from www.earlychildhoodaustralia.org.au/australianjournalofearlychildhood. Accessed 17 October 2013.

Van Ausdale, D. and Feagin, J. R. (2001) *The First R.: How Children Learn Race and Racism*. Lanham, Maryland, USA: Rowman and Littlefield.

1

CRITICAL RACE THEORY

A tool for understanding the racialisation of black children in education

Introduction

Challenges to racism in education are approached from diverse perspectives and understandings of black children's experiences in the classroom. However, although experiences are unique, some common underlying issues in the form of both institutional and interactional aspects of racism contribute to everyday life in the early years setting. Although often unintentional and misinterpreted, they must be recognised as creating an environment that contributes to the racialisation of black children. This chapter introduces Critical Race Theory (CRT) as a theoretical approach for interpretation of how these factors may operate through children's everyday interactions during their first introduction to an institutional culture that differs from that in their homes. Understanding their experiences through a CRT lens can allow for a greater insight into how possible discriminatory practices can be addressed. CRT accepts as a fundamental truth that racism is embedded in society and its institutions (Ladson-Billings and Tate IV, 2009). The term racialisation is used to describe processes whereby people are categorised based on socially constructed concepts of race. Racialisation is perpetuated not only through personal interactions but also through activity in institutional practices. Despite popular beliefs in their innocence and perceived lack of awareness of racial differences between people, children are not isolated from the effects of racialisation and related notions of power and privilege. By applying CRT precepts it is possible to challenge the complex and often subtle manifestations of race and racism that influence early education (Burdsey, 2011). CRT recognises the historical development of British society, such as slavery and colonisation, as having contributed to the inevitability of racism being present today across all areas of social policy and practice. Social and economic factors impact on young children's lives and their experiences in school. However, the premise that racism is present in both covert and overt forms does not mean that black children are inevitably prevented from accessing educational opportunities. CRT can inform professional and personal responsibilities to address racism and to support children's personal challenges to racialisation, as evidenced through their own stories in this book.

This chapter also discusses the concept of whiteness as a social construct and how this can be an important discriminatory factor in education, as it creates hierarchies of power that marginalise and other those who do not conform to the cultural norms of institutional ethos and practices. Whiteness is accompanied with what McIntosh (1997) refers to as an invisible knapsack of privileges that can go unrecognised by those who carry them. These advantages and the normalisation of whiteness are discussed here as contributing to inequalities in education. The CRT tenets discussed below are aimed at recognising the processes of racialisation that can stealthily marginalise black children. Listening to their voices through a CRT lens can contribute to the existing aims and action in the early years sector towards providing equality.

What is Critical Race Theory?

Critical Race Theory (CRT) emerged in the 1970s as a movement founded in American Critical Legal Studies (CLS) to address disadvantages in the legal system that disempower and discriminate against black people (Taylor, 2009; Yosso, 2005). During the 1960s, the civil rights movement in the United States protested against the unjust treatment of black people across America, resulting in legislative change through civil rights law. This was anticipated to be advantageous to the black community in creating a more equal society and signifying the end of racism. However, racism continued to disadvantage othered communities in all areas of American life. To further address this disadvantage, CRT was introduced as a race-conscious viewpoint within CLS to place race at the centre of legal analyses (Crenshaw, 1995). CRT was further applied in the 1980s to all areas of society through a multidisciplinary approach to centralise race in the challenge to inequalities (Delgado and Stefancic, 2001; Parker and Lynn, 2009). To challenge historically derived discrimination and racism in British society, CRT has recently been adapted to the UK context (Taylor et al., 2009; Hylton et al., 2009). Although the USA and the UK have different historical contexts regarding race relations, there are similarities in power relations between black and white populations as a consequence of slavery. Equality legislation in Britain has been in place since the 1976 Race Relations Act but has made little structural change to the lives of the black communities (MacGregor-Smith, 2017). CRT is applied to the UK context as a means to disrupt this continued disadvantage through centring race and racism in both education and other aspects of social policy as a main determinant in experiences of minority communities. CRT principles can enable a more direct approach to challenge elements that reproduce inequality in early years settings by focusing on the processes that reproduce disadvantage. Action can then be channelled away from personal locations to focus on structural discriminatory practices (Preston, 2009). Personal commitment to challenge racism can have minimal effect unless the institutional factors are also addressed. This can begin by acknowledging how children are racialised through both external and internal processes that reproduce disadvantage. Institutional factors in early years education that impact on inequalities can include pedagogy, curriculum, staffing and procedures for addressing racism.

A more equitable learning environment for young children can be possible by centralising race in policy decisions through a CRT framework that considers the historical, social and political contexts of young black children's experiences in early years education. We are all influenced by our generational histories with social factors, as well as racism at institutional and personal levels, contributing to barriers against equality in education. It is against a current background of increasing cuts in public services, rising unemployment, poverty and unequal housing policies that young British children bring their socio-cultural experiences to the early years setting. A CRT lens places importance on the historical experiences of racism to contextualise young black children's social worlds today in terms of their racialised identities, cultural stereotypes, and social and economic positions. Young children are living with the consequences of government policy on their families during processes of early socialisation when they begin to understand what it means to be black and British. This is discussed in Chapter 2 in relation to black children's identities within the current political context of what constitutes Britishness arising from introduction of the Prevent strategy (HMG, 2011). Young children's early education does not take place in isolation but is influenced by events that impact on families before birth and afterwards within an ecological niche which contextualises their lives (Aubrey et al., 2000). All aspects of children's social and economic lives have relevance to their formative years in education when placed in a cultural-historical context of race relations in the UK. The intersections of immigration status, gender, phenotype, sexuality and religion are all influencing factors on black children's cultures and identities (Yosso, 2005). Gender and phenotype feature strongly in the experiences of children in this book, as revealed in Devon's and Pina's stories (Chapters 3 and 5). Wright Jnr. describes the powerful impact of race on black children's lives as an overriding element:

> Race dominates our personal lives because it manifests itself in our speech, dance, neighbours and friends, and in our ways of talking, walking, eating and dreaming.
>
> *(1997, p. 321)*

The early formative experiences of black children are challenged through their initial relationships with the institutional whiteness of school. This ethos can deny the integral role of black people in society, which Fryer (1985) suggests has existed since the Roman invasion of the second century AD. During slavery and following abolition, black people continued to be part of English society across all classes and professions. It is rarely discussed that from 1885 Queen Victoria financially supported a young African girl and, later, her daughter throughout their education

(Myers, 1999). Queen Victoria's Asian goddaughter was a member of her court and active in the early suffragette movement. Aspects of British history that tell of past and present roles of the black population in British society are often excluded from the school curriculum, marginalising black communities as the other and alienating pupils through invisibility.

Attitudes in society to the black population in Britain are strongly influenced by government policy on immigration, employment, housing and economic factors. The development of immigration and race relations policies since the 1940s has impacted on the families of many black children currently in early years settings. Original settlers from the Caribbean who came to contribute to the rebuilding of Britain after the Second World War report how discrimination was evident during this period, in housing, employment and education (Phillips and Phillips, 1998). Assimilation was the emerging ideology in race relations during the 1950s as England became more ethnically and racially diverse. Assimilation can be defined as 'the attempt to eradicate, or at least reduce to an absolute minimum, signs of racial and cultural difference' (Gillborn, 2009, p. 73). Assimilation of diverse cultures was considered at the time as essential to the maintenance of the dominant culture, as affiliations through ethnicity could be seen to promote alternative group values that threaten traditional Britishness. An immigrant and generational black British youth emerged with economic disadvantage as racism established a barrier to assimilation into white cultural norms.

Integration became the revised policy shift of the 1970s in response to unrealistic expectations of assimilation through denial of cultural diversity. Integration aimed to provide for 'co-existence of minority cultures with the majority culture in a two-way process, each being of equal value and being equally respected' (Lane, 2008, p. 338). Integration requires acceptance of diverse cultures in society and willingness to live side by side, acknowledging differences positively, which is sometimes referred to as the 'melting pot' of British culture. This is where reified notions of cultural habitus are respected and valued as an 'exotic and interesting mix' when viewed from the accepted but undisrupted hierarchy of white cultural norms (Bradbury, 2013, p. 85).

Multiculturalism and cultural pluralism are coexistent terms applied within the race relations policy of integration. The terms describe intentional support for the right to maintain an independent cultural heritage while publically accepting and abiding by cultural norms established by the white indigenous population. Integration fails to address the structural aspects of racism in society, but rather promotes cultural differences through multiculturalism and harmonious relationships. This approach can further racialise communities by othering those who do not subscribe to cultural norms of a perceived traditional Britishness.

Cultural pluralism and multiculturalism assume commonality within fixed cultural definitions of homogenised groups. This essentialism denies colonial and postcolonial histories of immigrant communities and the development of emerging variations in cultural identities and experiences of racialisation within a concept of Britishness. Without recognition of discriminatory political, social and economic factors as barriers to equality, policies of meritocracy that place responsibility solely on the individual will continue to marginalise sections of the community. These discussions continue within the current debate that blames immigration for economic and social decline in Britain, contributing to the majority decision in 2016 for Britain to leave the European Union. Assimilation has been rephrased as Britishness with cultural diversity interpreted as a destructive element whereas it was historically welcomed in integration policy as being positive towards an inclusive British culture. Social and political factors contribute to the experiences of black children before they enter the early years setting. Multiculturalism can be argued as marginalising rather than including black children through an acceptance of whiteness as the norm in British culture, reproducing essentialist notions of cultural diversity and false stereotypes of their lives. Within a culturally hierarchical society such as Britain with a history of racism, CRT questions whether difference can be interpreted as positive and otherness equal without race and racism being central to the debate (Delgado and Stefancic, 2001).

The guiding principles of CRT towards an understanding of black children's experiences

CRT can provide a focus on how racism impacts on everyday personal interactions and systemic processes within early years institutions. Covert ways in which children are racialised through routines and the hidden curriculum should be considered when determining action to support black children such as those whose experiences form the rationale for this book. Anti-racist activity is facilitated by applying the precepts of CRT as a framework for analysis of children's experiences to understand the processes of racialisation that can impact on early education. CRT is not only a theoretical lens through which to observe and analyse early experiences in education, but it also demands action towards inclusive environments that challenge discriminatory processes. The guiding principles of CRT have no single definition as interpretations can vary according to differing contexts. However, Hylton offers a summary of the tenets that form the foundation of a CRT framework:

- The centralisation of race and racism.
- A transdisciplinary approach to CRT, which recognises the centrality of race and intersectionality of experience in relation to class, gender, ability, culture and religion.
- The centralisation of the marginalised voice.
- The challenge to traditional dominant ideologies around objectivity, meritocracy colour-blindness, race-neutrality and equal opportunities.
- A commitment to social justice, liberation and transformation.

(2009, pp. 29–36)

These tenets, although not exhaustive, form the basis of CRT praxis and are emerging as a useful framework for educational research and practice in England.

For further reading, Delgado and Stefancic (2001) provide an introduction to CRT that outlines and discusses the tenets and principles of CRT. This chapter focuses on those tenets that are the most relevant to contextualise, analyse and understand the experiences of the children who share their stories in this book.

Counter-narratives – the centralisation of race and racism in early years education through listening to the voices of black children

A primary tenet of CRT is acceptance that racism is endemic in society, and therefore all young children become aware of racism as they are exposed from birth to societal attitudes to race alongside other areas of discrimination. It is through interactions within families and wider communities that such understandings and attitudes form the foundations for new experiences. Omi and Winant (2005, p. 10) propose that as race is a socially constructed concept based partly on physical appearance, it is historically embedded in society and will determine hierarchies in social relationships despite contextual political, economic and social shifts. They see the concept of race operating as an inevitable and positive 'marker of the infinity of variations humans hold as a common heritage'. CRT facilitates an understanding of the lived, ever-changing realities of racism and how it continues historically in society to disadvantage sections of the British population and benefit others. By acknowledging how race and racism contribute to the social construction of black children's identities it is possible to explore the processes that impact on their education in a broader societal context.

Racism can be better understood through the CRT tenet of understanding the historically oppressed positions of those in society who are not generally heard in conjunction with empowering and including their views. Counter-narratives give a view of how racism is experienced to discriminate and marginalise minority groups in society from a position of racial realism. Narratives from privileged voices convey whiteness as the norm. This concept of the norm of Britishness reproduces existing dominant attitudes and societal status in relation to intersectional characteristics such as age, race, class, ability, sexual orientation and gender. By marginalising those who do not conform to ideas of the norm, the voices of those under-represented groups in racial hierarchies are often excluded, maintaining advantage for privileged groups. Narrative is a traditionally accepted method of collecting and representing data in research and is an important way of hearing the voices of otherwise silent groups such as young children. Gussin-Paley's (1998) use of narrative is a powerful tool to understand how young children interact when asserting their independence and agency through self-directed play activity. Representations through peer group relationships, play choices, problem-solving activity and creative media, as well as through their verbal interactions, show how experiences in the early years inform attitudes and dispositions to learning. Children's stories indicate how they are able to apply their socio-cultural experiences and understandings to the acquisition of new knowledge and perspectives during play and performances of racialised and gendered identities. Paley's counter-narratives challenge 'truths' such as young children not being developmentally able to understand issues of race and gender. They indicate that attitudes are not mimetic representations of societal values but that children are cognitively able to use racialised and gendered identities to maintain dominant hierarchies in their social worlds.

The counter-story as a form of narrative is a means to realistically reveal, examine and understand the perspectives of racialised individuals and communities. Counter-stories tell of the everyday experiences of the reality of racism, enabling marginalised communities to express their views and experiences. Counter-narratives were applied to challenge the lack of change in race relations following the civil rights action in the 1960s and currently convey the racialised experiences of communities across all sectors in society, including education. They are used extensively in CRT both in the USA (Dixson and Rousseau, 2006a) and in Britain (Rollock et al., 2015) as a means of empowering communities by identifying with experiences not usually voiced. This sharing of experiences reveals a contrasting reality, giving evidence to challenge the commonly accepted perspectives of the dominant white group. Counter-narratives used in CRT come in written and spoken forms such as biographies, autobiographies, personal accounts and other peoples' stories (Solorzano and Yosso, 2009). They can comprise data from both single and composite characters in real or fictional situations to tell of the lived experiences of othered communities. Bell's use of storytelling is developed in CRT through both fictional and non-fictional narratives, such as the Space Invaders. This fictional story illustrates the structural and political injustices against racialised groups operating through hierarchies of power (Bell, 1992). Warmington (2012) explains counter-narrative as a means by which alternative voices to those holding power in society can assert their 'agency, voice and history'. Opportunities to be heard not only counteract dominant views, but can also have a positive psychological impact through easing the stress and pain which racism inflicts (Delgado, 2000). A sharing of experiences through storytelling can provide solidarity with others to help understand and challenge racism and the impact it has on everyday lives. Confidence to take action for social and political change is then increased through acceptance of common experiences as the truth. This is in a context where the reality of racism told through counter-narratives is often questioned as false or exaggerated by those who do not experience racism.

Counter-narratives of young black children in the English education system can give insight into their unique experiences of being black in the white-dominated institutions of the school as well as empowering them through an alternative discourse (Dixson and Rousseau, 2006b). Reflexive interpretation of black children's experiences through their own stories can raise awareness of the hierarchies of what constitutes truth, better enabling the focus on their education from the children's perspectives. Early childhood research has historically ignored issues of race in research, and a CRT framework can address this omission by challenging the position that children are too developmentally immature to require a theoretical analysis of race and racism in the early years sector. This book contributes in a small capacity to achieving that aim through three composite narratives. The children's stories are compiled from research data of the seven participants. They are situated within a fictional timescale to represent the commonality and intensity of the experiences for many black children. Experiences of black children that are constructed through perspectives of whiteness can be challenged in relation to neutrality and objectivity by privileging the voices of black children, practitioners and parents. By listening to black children through their many forms of expression in daily activity and representing their voices in counter-narratives, opportunities are afforded for them to articulate their experiences. Meaning can be socially constructed in context with the unique lives of each individual, making it possible to challenge any preformed ideas or stereotypes of their experiences (Ladson-Billings, 2008). CRT tenets can be useful in this process to contextualise the children's stories by linking theory to practice through a critical lens, creating opportunities for action against discrimination in education. The counter-narratives of the black children in this book not only give them voice but can also raise awareness of the more covert racialising processes, thus motivating activism to address issues of power and privilege. A CRT framework for analysis that accepts and centralises race as an inevitable factor in black children's experiences can enable interpretation of their stories to focus on crucial issues of racialisation that impact on their education.

Whiteness as an element of CRT

Whiteness is an important precept in CRT through the scholarship of Critical White Studies and activism through White-Crit in the USA (Bell, 1997; Delgado and Stefancic, 2001; Ladson-Billings, 2006) and more recently in the UK (Leonardo, 2009; Preston, 2009; Gillborn, 2008). Whiteness is viewed in CRT as a socially constructed identity determined by the changing political and social context and not as a permanent biological state. There is often confusion between 'whiteness as a phenotype and whiteness as a hegemonic structure' (Preston and Chadderton, 2012, p. 88). It is more complex than a biological white/black concept that is used to racialise and exclude social groups. Whiteness can be better explained as a socially constructed identity to maintain the status quo. Those who do not generally think of themselves as a racialised group can perceive whiteness as the norm with the consequence that whiteness can become invisible to them and unchallenged while maintaining power and privilege through creating a sense of entitlement (Hylton, 2009, pp. 65–69). Political and personal definitions of whiteness are summarised by Sims and Lea as

> a complex, hegemonic and dynamic set of mainstream socio-economic processes and ways of thinking, feeling, believing and acting that function to obscure the power, privilege and practices of the social elite. . . . Whiteness

is the air we breathe: it is the mainstream waters of society in which we all, to a greater or lesser extent swim.

(2008a, p. 68)

Critical White Studies enables a focus on those processes in society responsible for reproducing racism through unequal power relations.

Whiteness dominates institutions such as schools to marginalise and disadvantage those who are not seen as being white. This can create a foundation for the conservation of privilege and racism in society. White-Crit as an activist element of CRT places responsibility on the white community to understand the construction of whiteness and its silent but powerful role in reproducing racism in education and society generally. Gillborn (2016) gives statistical evidence across a twenty-year period of black African-Caribbean underachieving through changes in assessment measures. Black students' experiences identify the numerous institutional factors that confirm whiteness as an accepted hierarchy in education. Gillborn's evidence contradicts evidence gained through statistics based on those entitled to free school meals to support current discourse that resources should be aimed at white working-class boys, as they are the highest group of underachieving pupils. This methodology excludes black boys who are not in this category, giving a simplistic analysis that evades discussion of race in education while maintaining a focus on whiteness. White-Crit aims to create an awareness of socially constructed processes of whiteness and the power and privilege that accompany them in order to challenge racism and the effects on othered communities.

The privileges afforded by whiteness are in personal, material and economic forms as well as at macro societal and political levels. McIntosh (1997) explains whiteness as a range of 'special provisions, assurances and blank checks' that are such an integral part of life for the white population that they go unnoticed and are taken for granted as the norm. Three of the fifty examples of her white privilege are as follows:

> I can easily buy posters . . . greeting cards, dolls, toys, and children's magazines featuring people of my own race. I do not have to educate my children to be aware of systemic racism for their own daily protection. I can be sure that my children will be given curricular materials that testify to the existence of their race.
>
> *(1997, p. 291)*

There is often a lack of awareness of how such advantages of whiteness contribute to social, political and economic status, discriminating against those who are not identified as white. Dawn's story (Chapter 6) is told in this book to highlight the importance of white practitioners being aware how their whiteness can influence the experiences of black children in education. An understanding of McIntosh's invisible knapsack of privileges and how whiteness can influence everyday actions that marginalise others is essential for action against discrimination and the racialisation of black children in education.

Whiteness as the norm in education

Paradigms in education such as multiculturalism and anti-racism have had little effect in addressing inequalities and the disaffection with school of some black children. Although anti-racist action has supported children at micro levels in the classroom, it has failed to make a lasting and positive impact on challenging structural racism in schooling. Initiatives such as multiculturalism and equality policy can be viewed by some as sufficient to challenge racism without viewing how whiteness can impact on inequalities. A lack of critical analysis can lead to blame being placed on children for non-conformity in the classroom, rather than seeing this as a possible challenge to their racialisation. Responsibility for change is then placed solely on the children themselves rather than on those professionals who maintain that school processes are already effective in promoting equality. Normative whiteness is acquired by white children from birth through verbal and non-verbal micro-messages conveyed in the home and wider community that instil the invisibility and normality of white power and privilege. This acceptance should be challenged as soon as white children enter school, as they have already been exposed to silences regarding racism and white privilege, contributing to unequal relationships with peers. Schools can be a major influence on the ideology of whiteness, as they provide early exposure for young black children through their interactions with peers alongside the institutional whiteness of the environment. Whiteness can determine the ethos of a school by acceptance of its normality, consciously or unconsciously grounded in white middle-class values to the exclusion of othered cultural norms. The whiteness of the traditional, Eurocentric classroom can be viewed as the dominant ethos through which British education policy and praxis is determined (Sims and Lea, 2008b). Chapter 2 explores in more detail how black children's early experiences in schools are influenced by unquestionable norms of whiteness and how they adapt by maintaining their black identities through psychological strategies such as Dubois' (1994) notion of 'double-consciousness' and Fanon's (2008) 'white masks'.

Gillborn (2008) argues that only when schools operate to understand how whiteness impacts on the education of black pupils will their interests be addressed and schooling become relevant for them. This includes creating awareness in staff teams of the normalisation of whiteness in institutions and working towards implementation of a relevant critical anti-racist praxis. CRT provides a framework for challenging the impact of racism in education through centralisation of race, to which the concept of whiteness as well as blackness is fundamental. Challenging racism through White-Crit is an alternative approach that examines how whiteness reproduces disadvantage for racialised communities. This is in contrast to the often pathological view of marginalised communities themselves reproducing their own disadvantage which has often led the theoretical discourses on racism (Manglitz, 2003). The impact of whiteness on black children in the reception classroom is discussed in this book through a white practitioner's lens (Chapter 6). Her story tells of how speaking with a black colleague raises an awareness of her own positioning of whiteness when interpreting a black child's experience of racialisation. It is easy for her to return to the comfort of white privilege when essential dialogue with colleagues is not maintained to question the dominance of whiteness that perpetuates her advantage.

Summary

Race is discussed in this chapter as an ever-present and additional, overarching discriminating factor within the intersections of other inequalities. CRT is the ideological frame applied to question dominant truths that may deny equality in early years education, such as the naivety of children to race and racism, and challenges to racism having no place in early years settings. CRT opposes liberal notions of equal opportunities and meritocracy, which see educational attainment as being possible through focus on individual responsibility without consideration of the institutional, social and political factors that impact on children's education. A colour-blind approach that considers all children as having equal opportunities can ignore those racialising processes that contribute to black children continuing to be marginalised through institutional practices. Social justice viewed through a CRT lens includes the intersections of experiences that impact on young children's education according to other factors such as gender and class.

Whiteness is considered in CRT as a barrier to equality and a means to perpetuate social and economic hierarchies based on the racialisation of diverse groups in society. Structural processes in institutions can result in discriminatory environments that advantage white communities to the exclusion of racialised others. It is the responsibility of those who benefit from whiteness to question personal perspectives as well as how practices and procedures in social, education and economic arenas can disadvantage some through racialised hierarchies. Hearing counter-narratives told by those whose experiences are under-represented and often interpreted as false are an important way of de-centring from positions of whiteness. The intersections of race, gender, ability and age can marginalise black voices in the early years classroom. By allowing time for children to tell their stories, practitioners can understand how children adopt strategies to adjust to the new world of education. By listening to children's voices, their experiences make apparent how identities are challenged in their everyday interactions and how their education is influenced by the whiteness of the classroom. Chapter 2 explores this further through concepts applied in CRT that contribute to the racialisation of black children's identities.

Reflective practice

- Do your procedures for communicating with parents and carers consider the varying cultural, social and economic circumstances of families? How can your procedures facilitate communication with parents without being intrusive?
- How can you provide diverse opportunities for children to tell and for practitioners to hear their stories?

- Does your setting reflect the diversity of a British identity through resources and displays? How can you challenge any predominance of whiteness in procedures and practices?

References

Aubrey, C., David, T., Godfrey, R. and Thompson, L. (eds.) (2000) *Early Childhood Educational Research: Issues in Methodology and Ethics.* London: Routledge Falmer.

Bell, D. A. (1992) *Faces at the Bottom of the Well: The Permanence of Racism.* New York, USA: Basic Books.

Bell, D. A. (1997) White Supremacy (And What We Should Do about It), in Delgado, R. and Stefancic, J. (eds.), *Critical White Studies.* Philadelphia, USA: Temple University Press.

Bradbury, A. (2013) *Understanding Early Years Inequality: Policy, Assessment and Young Children's Identities.* Oxon: Routledge.

Burdsey, D. (2011) Applying a CRT Lens to Sport in the UK: The Case of Professional Football, in Hylton, K., Pilkington, A., Warmington, P. and Housee, S. (eds.), *Atlantic Crossing: International Dialogues on Critical Race Theory.* Birmingham: C-SAP the Higher Education Academy Network.

Crenshaw, K. (1995) Intersections of Race and Gender. In Crenshaw, K. Gotanda, N. Pella G. and Thomas, K. eds. *Critical Race Theory: The Key Writings that formed the Movement.* New York: The New Press.

Delgado, R. (2000) Storytelling for Oppositionists and Others: A Plea for Narrative, in Delgado, R. and Stefancic, J. (eds.), *Critical Race Theory: The Cutting Edge,* 2nd ed. Philadelphia, USA: Temple University Press.

Delgado, R. and Stefancic, J. (2001) *Critical Race Theory, an Introduction.* New York, USA: New York State University Press.

Dixson, A. and Rousseau, C. (2006a) The First Day of School: A CRT Story, in Dixson, A. and Rousseau, C. (eds.), *Critical Race Theory in Education.* Oxon: Routledge.

Dixson, A. and Rousseau, C. (2006b) And We Are Still Not Saved, in Dixson, A. and Rousseau, C. (eds.), *Critical Race Theory in Education.* Oxon: Routledge.

DuBois, W. E. B. (1994) *The Souls of Black Folk.* New York, USA: Dover Publications.

Fanon, F. (2008) *Black Skins, White Masks.* London: Pluto Press.

Fryer, P. (1985) *Staying Power.* London: Pluto Press.

Gillborn, D. (2008) *Racism and Education, Coincidence or Conspiracy.* Oxon: Routledge.

Gillborn, D. (2009) Education Policy as an Act of White Supremacy, in Taylor, E., Gillborn, D. and Ladson-Billings, G. (eds.), *Foundations of Critical Race Theory in Education.* Oxon: Routledge.

Gillborn, D. (2016) *White Lies: Things That Were Told about Race and Education That Weren't True.* Available from www.birmingham.ac.uk/schools/education/research/2016/gillborn. Accessed 10 January 2017.

Gussin-Paley, V. (1998) *The Girl with the Brown Crayon.* Cambridge, MA, USA: Harvard University Press.

Her Majesty's Government (HMG) (2011) *Prevent Strategy.* London: The Stationary Office.

Hylton, K. (2009) *'Race' and Sport, Critical Race Theory.* Oxon: Routledge.

Hylton, K., Pilkington, A., Warmington, P. and Housee, S. (eds.) (2009) *Atlantic Crossing: International Dialogues on Critical Race Theory.* Birmingham: C-SAP the Higher Education Academy Network.

Ladson-Billings, G. (2006) Foreword, in Dixson, A. and Rousseau, C. (eds.), *Critical Race Theory in Education.* Oxon: Routledge.

Ladson-Billings, G. (2008) Fighting for Our Lives: Preparing Teachers to Teach African American Students, in Darder, A., Baltodano, M. and Torres, R. (eds.), *The Critical Pedagogy Reader*, 2nd ed. Oxon: Routledge.

Ladson-Billings, G. and Tate IV, W. F. (2009) Toward a Critical Race Theory of Education, in Darder, A., Baltodano, M. and Torres, R. (eds.), *The Critical Pedagogy Reader*, 2nd ed. Oxon: Routledge.

Lane, J. (2008) *Young Children and Racial Justice*. London: National Children's Bureau.

Leonardo, Z. (2009) *Race, Whiteness and Education*. Oxon: Routledge.

MacGregor-Smith, R. (2017) *Race in the Workplace, the MacGregor-Smith Review*. Available from www.gov.uk>publications>race-in-the-workplace. Accessed 18 December 2017.

Manglitz, E. (2003) Challenging White Privilege in Adult Education: A Critical Review of the Literature, in *Adult Education Quarterly*, 2 (53) pp. 119–134.

McIntosh, P. (1997) White Privilege and Male Privilege: A Personal Account of Coming to See Correspondences through Work in Women's Studies, in Delgado, R. and Stefancic, J. (eds.), *Critical White Studies, Looking Behind the Mirror*. Philadelphia, USA: Temple University Press.

Myers, W. D. (1999) *At Her Majesty's Request: An African Princess in Victorian England*. USA: Scholastic.

Omi, M. and Winant, H. (2005) The Theoretical Status of the Concept of Race, in Critchlow, W., Dimitriadi, G. and Dolby (eds.), *Race, Identity and Representation in Education*. Oxon: Routledge.

Parker, L. and Lynn, M. (2009) What's Race Got to Do with It?, in Taylor, E., Gillborn, D. and Ladson-Billings, G. (eds.), *Foundations of Critical Race Theory in Education*. Oxon: Routledge.

Phillips, M. and Phillips, T. (1998) *The Windrush: Irresistible Rise of Multi-Ethnic Britain*. UK: Harper Collins.

Preston, J. (2009) *Whiteness and Class in Education*. London: Springer.

Preston, P. and Chadderton, C. (2012) Rediscovering 'Race Traitor': Towards a Critical Race Theory Informed Public Pedagogy, in *Race Ethnicity and Education*, 15 (1) pp. 85–100.

Rollock, N., et al. (2015) *The Colour of Class*. Oxon: Routledge.

Sims, E. J. and Lea, V. (2008a) Transforming Whiteness through Poetry, in Sims, E. J. and Lea, V. (eds.), *Undoing Whiteness in the Classroom*. New York, USA: Peter Lang.

Sims, E. J. and Lea, V. (2008b) Imagining Whiteness Hegemony in the Classroom: Undoing Oppressive Practice and Inspiring Social Justice Activism, in Sims, E. J. and Lea, V. (eds.), *Undoing Whiteness in the Classroom*. New York, USA: Peter Lang.

Solorzano, G. and Yosso, T. (2009) Critical Race Methodology: Counter-Storytelling as an Analytical Framework for Educational Research, in Taylor, E., Gillborn, D. and Ladson-Billings, G. (eds.), *Foundations of Critical Race Theory in Education*. Oxon: Routledge.

Taylor, E. (2009) Critical Race Theory and Interest Convergence in the Backlash against Affirmative Action, in Taylor, E., Gillborn, D. and Ladson-Billings, G. (eds.), *Foundations of Critical Race Theory in Education*. Oxon: Routledge.

Taylor, E., Gillborn, D. and Ladson-Billings, G. (eds.) (2009) *Foundations of Critical Race Theory in Education*. Oxon: Routledge.

Warmington, P. (2012) 'A Tradition in Ceaseless Motion': Critical Race Theory and Black British Intellectual Spaces, in *Race, Ethnicity and Education*, 15 (1) pp. 5–21.

Wright, L., Jnr. (1997) Race and Racial Classification, in Delgado, R. and Stefancic, J. (eds.), *Critical White Studies: Looking Behind the Mirror*. Philadelphia, USA: Temple University Press.

Yosso, T. (2005) Whose Culture Has Capital? A Critical Race Theory Discussion of Community Cultural Wealth, in *Race, Ethnicity and Education*, 8 (1) pp. 69–91.

2

KEY INFLUENCES ON BLACK CHILDREN'S IDENTITIES

Introduction

When children enter early years settings they build on their early identities formed in the home by responding to interactions in the new environment. School can be the initial place where black children are alone in their experiences of racialisation as they enter a world outside the home and immediate community. They will need to adjust to cultural norms that differ from those to which they are accustomed. Learning new ways of socialising in an institutional environment can cause conflict and create additional pressures on young children as they attempt to meet unfamiliar expectations. For black children this can mean adapting to a whiteness that may marginalise their identities. Children are perceived from diverse perspectives as a consequence of new relationships with practitioners and peers, as well as by their responses to the structural aspects and expectations of the school, such as the curriculum, policies and procedures. Environmental interactions can marginalise and other young black children through intentional and unintentional, institutional or personal racism. The impact on their identities can create a sense of exclusion that influences future dispositions to school and education generally. Such exposure can result in feelings of 'humiliation, isolation and self-hatred' in young children that can be psychologically damaging if not acknowledged and supported (Delgado, 2000, p. 132). Reflective early years practice can provide an environment where racialising factors that influence their early experiences can be addressed by an understanding of how these processes operate. Children are capable of developing mature countering strategies with which they resist challenges to their black identity from a young age, contesting the false conception of their naivety and innocence regarding race and racism in their lives (Van Ausdale and Feagin, 2001). Peer group friendships are discussed in this chapter as one means by which to support these challenges as children understand how to conform to accepted school norms of whiteness. Some develop a parallel identity, which DuBois (2009) refers to as a double-consciousness, for support through the processes of assuming learner identities that are accepted as positive. This chapter discusses concepts applied within CRT, such as micro-aggressions and colour-blindness, and how they impact on young black children's identities in order to better understand the implications of racism on their early experiences.

Influences on young black children's identities as they enter school

All children are likely to enter school with racialised identities formed in their homes through exposure to racism in their communities and by hearing and participating in adult conversations. As children's worlds extend out of the home they are further exposed to powerful negative images and stereotypes of blackness portrayed through the media and everyday interactions. These verbal and visual assaults confirm hierarchical values of whiteness as an identity with the processes of racialisation in the classroom contributing to perceptions of themselves. The developmental approach in the EYFS curriculum guidance and assessment procedures can disregard learned preformed attitudes through explaining children's understanding of race and racism as inaccurate due to cognitive immaturity, thus seeing bias as naturally disappearing as children mature cognitively (MacNaughton, 2003; Robinson and Jones Diaz, 2006). There can be a disregard to address racism both with children and in the hidden curriculum in favour of a tokenistic multicultural approach that further marginalises othered communities, as discussed in Chapter 7. The traditional approach in early years education is to nurture young children's development while viewing them as innocent and in need of protection; this makes recognition of racist attitudes more difficult to accept (Brown, 1998). Belief that raising issues of racism can damage young children's naivety and purity can be a barrier to establishing a critical consciousness of how children are racialised from a young age (Baldock, 2011). A reflective pedagogy that takes account of factors that racialise black children can support positive black identities formed in the home during this time of transition to new cultural expectations.

Children's understanding of hierarchies of whiteness in social relationships is indicated in early research in the USA that denoted children's preference of white or black dolls (Clark and Clark, 1947) and in England during the 1970s (Milner, 1975, 1983). Milner was influential in promoting the idea that black children may develop a low self-esteem from a young age through stereotypes of black people as inferior and marginalised as a group in society. Similar research into black children's identities was repeated in England for the BBC television series *A Child of Our Time* (BBC, 2005). Four-year-old children were asked to indicate whom they would choose as friends using photographs of white and black children rather than the dolls used in the earlier research. The majority of children selected the white child, giving negative responses about black children when questioned. The validity of these research projects has been questioned, as they take place in controlled environments rather than through natural observation of children in their play environment. Research findings of low self-esteem have been contested as a reason for white doll preference, with the major factor influencing children's preferences being internalisation of the hierarchical superiority of whiteness and marginalisation of blackness (Stone, 1981). The whiteness of the researchers has also been identified as a possible influence on preferences, as children have possibly already internalised the benefits of conforming to expectations of white practitioners as they adjust to the hierarchy of white norms in the setting. Davis (2007), a black researcher, reproduced the doll experiments with both white and black children. Fifteen of the twenty-one children preferred the white doll, with many referring to the black doll as 'bad'. Children's choices were made regardless of the racial designation of the researcher, indicating that racialised attitudes would appear to be the main influence on white doll preference. Davis concluded that stereotypes and racialisation of the black community are reflected in the doll choices of her young participants as they internalise negativity regarding black identities.

An aspect of the hidden curriculum is the omission of culturally relevant content and resources, which can also influence black children's self-perceptions. Absence of resources reflecting their cultural identity can result in black children being excluded and othered from the learning environment. Books, visual aids, computer programmes and imaginative play resources are all aspects of the hidden curriculum in early years settings. They are examples of how institutional policy can unintentionally filter into classroom pedagogy to marginalise black children's identities through the domination of whiteness. The hidden curriculum can be challenged through learning environments that represent all children alongside a critical pedagogy that recognises the strong influence of whiteness.

Identity and double-consciousness

As well as identifiable images through appropriate resourcing in the environment, other aspects of culture that are frequently ignored in the classroom should be considered. Language is used differently in school, and codes of behaviour can differ from those in the home. When conforming to new expectations children can become confused if exposed to negative concepts of their home cultures through omission of that which is familiar to them. Delgado proposes that there can follow an unquestioned acceptance of the school norms that infers a hierarchy of white culture, contributing to double-consciousness, which he explains as

> the propensity of excluded people to see the world in terms of two perspectives at the same time – that of the majority race, according to which they are demoralised, despised and reviled and their own, in which they are normal.
> *(2000, p. 389)*

When displays and resources only represent the majority population and culture, children who do not see themselves or their cultures in the classroom environment can feel marginalised and undervalued. Predominant whiteness in resources and the lack of representation of black identities can contribute to the 'unquestionable acceptance' of white norms. This cultural hierarchy may result in black children internalising a secondary identity framed by whiteness that is contradictory to their initial conception of being black. This process of identifying with the white norms of a setting is akin to children putting on a 'white mask', conforming to expectations around them whilst having to hide their true identity behind the 'mask' (Fanon, 2008). It can be removed when back in the familiar cultural environment of home and community. Wilson suggests that attending school for the first time 'for the black child is often a schizoid process' as children are alienated from their home through expectations to think, feel and behave in ways quite different from everyday life. They must

> maintain a precarious psychic balance between a black and white world, belonging to neither. To the black children, white middle class, institutional demands may seem unreasonable, unjust and unnecessary.
>
> *(1978, p. 186)*

The psychological effects of contradictions felt by children as they understand their relationship to the classroom culture can induce tensions that inevitably place additional pressures on them as they settle into school. Exposure to racialised ideology through institutional and personal factors in school may mean that children begin to see themselves as defined through the eyes of the dominant culture that portrays them as the out-group in society.

For young children, exposure to negative definitions of their identities can result in a conflict that may impact on their motivation to learn and generally participate in activities. Racialised stereotypes may determine how children reassess their cultural identities with respect to institutional codes of behaviour and conformity to whiteness. Particular groups of pupils may be racialised and gendered in the early years classroom as good pupils while others are viewed as unable to conform to expectations based on middle-class norms, whiteness and negative cultural stereotypes (Bradbury, 2013). This process that begins in the early years can continue throughout school life, compounding the psychological effects of living in two worlds (DuBois, 2009). A head teacher in this study recognised the need for all staff, including managers, to understand how racism impacts on all aspects of school life:

> It has to be a whole school ethos . . . understanding by senior people what racism really is and acting upon it so it is supported and eradicated as far as you can.

She acknowledges that racism is ever-present in society but that schools should be aware of their responsibility to provide an ethos through which this is challenged to provide a more inclusive learning environment. Dawn's story (Chapter 6) indicates how practitioners can be unaware of the impact of whiteness on black pupils and the importance of a critical approach to challenge the invisibility of racism and the consequences for their education.

Identity and racial micro-aggressions

Alongside double-consciousness, the concept of racial micro-aggressions is adopted in CRT to explain the everyday effects of often covert, unintentional racist inter-actions on the formation of black identity and psychological well-being (Davis, 2000). Racial micro-aggressions are 'subtle, automatic or unconscious racial insults' made during daily interactions (Dixson and Rousseau, 2006, p. 36). These insults can impact on the education of black children as they internalise the racialisation processes within institutional practices. Micro-aggressions can result in

> harmful psychological consequences . . . [that] sap the spiritual energies of recipients, lead to low self-esteem, and deplete or divert energy for adaptive functioning and problem solving.
>
> *(Sue, 2010, p. 15)*

They can be explained as acts of either intentional or unintentional assaults on minority groups performed by the white majority population who hold power in society and social institutions. They can be performed against any marginalised groups classified in terms such as gender, class, race, disability, sexual orientation and ethnicity. The children's stories in this book tell how racial micro-aggressions contribute to their racialisation, as discussed in analysis of their stories. Sue describes three main categories of racial micro-aggressions:

- Micro-insults – communications that convey rudeness and insensitivity and demean a person's racial heritage.
- Micro-assaults – explicit racial derogations characterised primarily by a violent verbal, nonverbal or environmental attack meant to hurt the intended vic-tim through name calling, avoidant behaviour or purposeful discriminatory actions.
- Micro-invalidations – Communications that exclude, negate, or nullify the psychological thoughts, feelings or experiential reality of a person of color.

(2010, p. 29)

Micro-aggressions can impact on early stages in children's identity formation through verbal and non-verbal interactions. Pina's story (Chapter 5) tells of how a micro-insult against her personal appearance has consequences on her actions in response to the racialisation of her black identity. Racial micro-invalidations may be evident in an early years context when aspects of black children's identity con-tradict institutional expectations: for example, when children use home languages and dialects in the school that are not accepted. Support in the early years for lan-guages spoken in the home is generally viewed as good practice, with fluency in any language recognised as an important step towards acquisition of English as a common form of verbal communication (Drury, 2007). As far as possible, the four schools in the study employ practitioners who speak the home languages of the children and encourage communication with peers using shared languages during play activity. Despite support for home languages, dialects spoken by children with an African-Caribbean heritage are not always valued in the same way. This is indicated by Devon and Neil (Chapter 3), who rap and use Jamaican dialect only when outside the hearing of practitioners. Pina and Remmie use dialect together in the playground and Pina speaks dialect to herself when alone during her café play (Chapter 5). Jason also speaks in dialect with peers from similar cultural heritages in the playground. He is observed whispering comments to himself during group times and when alone, self-narrating his construction play. Children in the study do not appear confident in using dialect when communicating with adults or children who are not from the same cultural background. This indicates a micro-invalidation that does not directly forbid or devalue their dialect in school, but is understood by the children as unacceptable through attitudes in society to the use of Caribbean dialects. Children transpose societal value of their dialects to unspoken expectations in school regarding acceptable use of language.

Both micro-insults and micro-invalidations are directed personally towards an Asian girl as she eats her lunch at a table with other children who have brought their lunches from home. She eats meat and rice with her fingers from a plastic container while other children eat sandwiches and wraps. Two boys at the table not only comment that her food is smelly, but also that her hands are dirty as they are stained by the food. This went unheard by the lunch supervisor, leaving the girl unsupported after the psychological impact of having her cultural practice invalidated. The convention of using a knife and fork to eat school meals can be an unrecognised micro-invalidation of children's usual cultural practices within the institutional perspectives of the predominant cultural norms that underpin regulations. Such comments made by the boys can induce negative impressions of what is already understood by children as positive aspects of their home cultures. A direct consequence of a micro-invalidation is when a 2-year-old child of African heritage attending a nursery was considered to be autistic because she would not sit at the table to eat but wandered the room with her food. The concern for formal assessment was discussed with her mother, who angrily informed practitioners that this was the custom during mealtimes at home and that her child should not be assessed without further evidence of autism or knowledge of her home culture. An unquestioned cultural hierarchy of the setting can marginalise those children who are not supported in adapting to new mealtime customs and can contribute to negative impacts on identity and psychological well-being.

Micro-assaults can occur through more overt forms of racism, such as direct racist insults and name-calling. The use of overt racist language is now challenged in schools since the introduction of the RRA Act 2000 and action is required to record and challenge racist language. However, micro-assaults still occur in children's interactions when adults are absent. When young children are developmentally able to use language to voice their feelings and opinions they verbally express learned attitudes that can give white children permission to call black children racist names (Brown, 2001). An example of this is when an Asian boy is reprimanded in school for calling a black girl by the N-word. The boy and his family meet confidentially with a practitioner on three occasions to discuss attitudes to race and the unacceptable use of racist terminology. However, the girl was not supported for the effects of the term, leading to possible acceptance of a right to assault her identity.

Racialised stereotypes of black children being good at music and sport can produce well-meaning compliments from both peers and adults. However, assumptions of innate skills assigned through biological definitions of 'race' and determining ability contribute to the supposition that black children have specific but non-academic skills. These racialised stereotypes may be internalised by some black children to adjust to cultural expectations in school where they attempt to conform by developing these attributes, rather than those in more academically valued subjects (Sewell, 2010). Acceptance of the centrality of race to black children's experiences can give insight into the impact of seemingly inoffensive comments given during everyday interactions from a perspective of whiteness. It is then possible to provide appropriate and effective support for black children to overcome invalidation of their true selves and assaults on their identities based on deterministic views of 'race'. The following examples of micro-aggressions tell of how learned racialised attitudes of identity are unintentionally conveyed to black children during play with peers. The first is a micro-invalidation of a black boy's positive black identity when he is chosen by his white peers to be the monster, giving him a stick to frighten them with while they run away from him. This indicates possible negative stereotypes acquired through media representations of black being bad and threatening. Negative connotations of black in society are constantly reinforced through forms of verbal and non-verbal micro-aggressions that contribute to the racialisation of black children's identities. Conversely, in the superhero play of a group of children, white boys are more often in charge, reflecting media images of a white hierarchy in relationships. Seemingly insignificant non-verbal micro-invalidations can impact on identity formation through unintentional actions in the classroom that discriminate against children. Black children are sometimes not included during group sessions even when they conform to expectations such as raising their hands to answer when teachers ask the group questions. Sonic has this experience when only selected on one occasion despite enthusiastically raising his hand throughout the session (Chapter 4). Although Sonic conforms to expectations of sitting cross-legged in the group, constant raising of the hand can be perceived as disruptive behaviour. Sonic continues to follow group rules, although reactions to not being chosen may result in some children not conforming, perpetuating the stereotype of disruptive black boys from the age of 5 (Wright, 1992). Micro-aggressions can go unnoticed by busy practitioners while impacting on black children's identities through the 'drip, drip effect' of numerous actions experienced as everyday racism (Essed, 2013).

In addition to micro-aggressions experienced through personal contact with others in social and educational contexts, children can experience those conveyed through institutional practices. The hidden curriculum and multiculturalism are discussed in Chapter 7 to highlight ways in which black children may be unintentionally marginalised. Sue uses the term environmental micro-aggressions to refer to these processes he describes as

> numerous demeaning and threatening social, educational, political, or economic cues that are communicated individually, institutionally, or societally to marginalised groups. Environmental micro-aggressions may be delivered visually or from a stated philosophy such as colour-blindness.
>
> *(2010, p. 25)*

Colour-blindness can be explained as an approach to equal opportunities through denial and minimising consequences of race and racism in education in favour of a view of equality, which is interpreted as treating everyone the same (Constantine and Sue, 2007). The denial of difference can permeate the ethos of the school when organising the curriculum and the visual environment and formulating institutional policies and procedures. By prioritising perspectives of the predominant class and race of staff and managers, important aspects of identity can be marginalised. In his research Sue (2010) gives a rationale for student teachers adopting a colour-blind stance as enabling them to ignore race and racial differences in classroom dialogues so as to avoid feeling uncomfortable in challenging them. It also allows them to maintain a view that they are unbiased and do not discriminate, avoiding difficult challenges and resulting in perpetuation of the power and privilege that comes with whiteness (Sleeter, 2005). This is likely to apply to those who may not acknowledge that racism can exist in young children and so can deny the impact on their experiences. Konstantoni (2013) found in her research with reception class teachers that the mantra for addressing incidents of racism between children was 'but we're all the same here', indicating a colour-blind approach. A colour-blind approach to classroom interactions with practitioners and in teaching methods can result in black children's experiences from home being excluded from the curriculum, as they may not be considered or else may be seen as inappropriate. Opportunities are then missed for connections between play and experiences at home, which children find valuable in the expression of their cultural identities. Yosso (2005) terms this as cultural wealth to describe the breadth of experience gained in the home and community that may not be valued in relation to the dominant white European culture in schools. Dismissal of cultural wealth through the predetermined norms of whiteness marginalises the importance of black children's personal experiences. These environmental micro-aggressions can add to the psychological impact on children's identity formation that is likely to go unidentified within colour-blind approaches.

The intersections of gender and race in young children's identities

The intersections of racialised and gendered identities create stereotypes of black masculinity that contrast with those of black female sexuality and compliance (hooks, 1993; Weiler, 2009). In the same manner in which experiences of racism contribute to a racialised identity, patriarchy reproduces a strong gender identity from an early age (Zamudio et al., 2011). A central tenet of CRT places intersectionality as pivotal in the contextual conflicts of race, class, gender and other socially determined discriminatory aspects of identity formation and psychological development (Winant, 2009; Crenshaw, 2009). Through this precept a view can be taken of the inevitability of young black children's exposure to a range of stereotypes and micro-aggressions depending on their positioning in diverse intersections. CRT proposes that a colour-blind approach to the experiences of black girls and women operates to marginalise their gendered experiences through comparison with white women's experiences of patriarchy that excludes their racialised black identities and contributes to disadvantage (Crenshaw, 1993; Harris, 2000). From the perspective of race as a primary factor in identification, intersections of race and gender can operate to discriminate against black girls and women differently to those who are white. Gender and race are not fixed separate categories. They interact with one another in the complexity of young children's identity formation through exposure to gendering alongside racialising experiences in their social worlds (Vaught and Hernandez, 2013).

Secondary socialisation begins when children start school and their identity is impacted through contextual interactions with peers based on already internalised conceptions of race and gender. As with race, where whiteness becomes invisible, with gender males do not always recognise the privileges of their masculinity within society, taking them for granted in a gendered hierarchy. Through interactions with both adults and peers, young children can accept dominant stereotypes of masculinity as right and true, making them difficult to challenge in the classroom context (Browne, 2004). Gendered and racialised stereotypes can then become integral to early stages of identity formation and result in behaviour and attitudes in school representing the perceived stereotypes. In one school that children in this book attend, boys and girls line up separately when leaving the classroom, reinforcing gender differences rather than contesting stereotypes. Kylie (Chapter 4), although not participating in the game, challenges the stereotype of only boys being interested in football by getting involved as the referee. Play choices made in the early years environment indicate gender identity through spaces occupied by either girls or boys. Common examples familiar to many practitioners are in the home play of girls and the more physical construction play of boys. Girls take ownership of the home play area, with boys recognising the gender hierarchy by perhaps taking a subordinate role to be accepted in the play. This may be as the baby, a cat or a docile husband and father. Alternatively girls may accept male dominance in the block play by playing alongside or in cooperation with boys' organisation of constructions. These gender stereotypical roles are challenged predominantly through intervention from practitioners. Young children construct their identities in context with gendered and racialised discourses of both peers and adults. Particular groups of pupils are frequently racialised and gendered in the early years as 'good pupils' while others are viewed as unable to conform to norms of behaviour and accepted attitudes (Brooker, 2010; Bradbury, 2013). Common stereotypes portray young black girls as compliant and collaborative in contrast to black boys, who may be seen as more aggressive and competitive, causing greater conflict between peers. These stereotypes can reflect the types of activity that children engage in, with girls choosing collaborative interactive teaching dependent on sharing ideas with peers and adults. Boys can favour more product-orientated work with didactic outcomes in tasks measured competitively against peers, such as block play and much outdoor play (Askew and Ross, 1998). Kylie's and Sonic's story (Chapter 4) illustrates how common stereotypes can influence behaviours. Kylie contrives to sit with a practitioner in a creative activity rather than in a group teaching session and remains close to her during outdoor play. Sonic plays actively with groups of boys and has little contact with practitioners other than in formal lessons.

Robinson and Jones Diaz (2006) suggest that although practitioners accept that young children internalise gender-appropriate behaviour from a young age, the use of power in gendered relationships is believed to be a complex adult concept which young children are developmentally incapable of understanding. Denial through blaming cognitive immaturity de-politicises gender and race in hierarchical power relations when it is considered as merely mimetic or immature repetition of adult behaviours. Divergence from gendered and racialised conformity in peer group relationships can result in being ostracised and bullied by peers. For black children the intersections of gendered and racialised identities can increase pressures to accept white peer group expectations of behaviour. Askew and Ross (1998) found that although some black children submit to racist behaviour to gain acceptance in the white group, other children attempt to resist exclusion. This can be through strategies such as not outwardly reacting to racial micro-aggressions, withdrawing from the group, forming their own racially exclusive groups or retaliating with abusive language. In Chapter 3 Devon resists verbal exclusion by playing alongside a group of white boys while returning abuse. His story also tells how friendships support black children as they use their agency to manage experiences of racialisation in the reception classroom.

Identity and peer group friendships

As children begin school, the dominance of whiteness can reflect on friendship choices of young black children who may feel marginalised. The research using dolls discussed in this chapter indicates that when adjusting to the white world of the classroom black children may seek an affirmation of acceptance through friendship choices, reflecting a dominant hierarchy of whiteness. These friendships do not necessarily reflect a low self-esteem but may be a positive means by which to understand the school culture. This understanding may be necessary for black children to make compromises, supporting them to inhabit comfortably the two different worlds of home and school (DuBois, 1994). The majority of boys in the research spoke of a white peer as their 'best friend' and chose their pseudonyms in relation to their friend's name. Cross-racial friendships can be a means by which black children acquire social skills necessary to adapt to the cultural anomalies in school (Graham et al., 1998). Support gained from white friends during this early process of socialisation can reduce stress and tensions created by the cultural conflicts of the classroom. If black children remain hidden in the environment either through the curriculum or representation in everyday interactions, then friendships with white peers can further minimise the importance and maintenance of a black identity. This can lead to temporary negation of their identities and cultures through a 'white mask' worn in school and discarded outside when secure in their black identities at home and in their communities (Fanon, 2008). In contrast to the boys in this study, same-race friendships have been found to be more common than interracial ones across all stages in education but particularly between 4-year-olds (Moody, 2001; McGlothlin, 2004). The importance of relationships with other black children can be considered as affirming identity and cultural experiences when confronted with challenges to their blackness. This is possible for Pina (Chapter 5) when during playtimes, she seeks out the only other girl in the reception classes who has the same racialised identity as herself. McGlothlin (2004) explains these challenges to identity as a result of stereotyping of the out-group within the hierarchy of white as good and smart, contrasting with black as bad. Same-race friendships can also be a means to identify common experiences and gain emotional and psychological support when exposed to the stereotyping and othering of a black identity. The experiences of girls in this book indicate that they are not as dependent as the boys on white friendships to conform to expectations, as they use their agency independently to challenge marginalisation.

Parental attitudes can also influence children's same-race friendship choices through personal, social preferences in their relationships with other adults. This is often a factor in choice of schools, either through recommendations from friends, or the reputations of schools reflecting similarities in race, culture, religion and class of families (Rollock et al., 2015). Relationships between children can develop according to similar cultural and racialised characteristics as they are encouraged by parents to attend the same out-of-school activities. As an inevitability of early socialisation and levels of independence, young children tend to adopt the racialised attitudes of their parents regarding who are deemed as suitable friends. Attitudes are conveyed to children through invitations into the home for play dates and through children's perceptions of the relationships between parents of peers with similar cultural and social backgrounds. Devon (Chapter 3) has been invited to his white friend Alan's home to play, perhaps strengthening their relationship across racialised boundaries. Friendships can be developed further in the classroom through common out-of-school experiences that can extend play in school. Socio-cultural aspects of play initiated through these shared experiences may also act to exclude peers, thus creating in- and out-friendship groups (Broadhead and Burt, 2012). The hidden curriculum might also influence friendship choices through unintentionally stereotyping black children as being good at particular activities such as sport and music and not sharing the same interests as their white peers.

There is very limited research on the implications of young children's friendship choices to promote greater understanding of the importance of this to racialisation of black children in schools. One reason proposed for the gap in recent relevant research on young children's attitudes to race and the impact on identity formation is that it is a highly contested field and there is a reluctance to acknowledge that young children can have racist attitudes (Robinson and Jones Diaz, 2006). This can lead to a situation where discussions of racism may be mistakenly thought to raise issues in children's minds that have not previously been present (Hart, 2009). A belief that they are too young to understand is apparent in a promotional transmission for children's television. Young children are interviewed with their best friends emphasising their closeness despite differences in various choices they voice in activities and food. The interviews are aimed to indicate a disregard of their apparent diversity in aspects of race, gender and disability and an unawareness of the 'isms' that accompany their identities. It has been demonstrated that the environment they find themselves in can have seriously detrimental effects on identity and feelings of self-worth that need to be raised and discussed as an integral aspect of their development (Brown, 2008). For these reasons the impact of racism on black children's identity can be better understood through recognition and critical interpretation that places race and racism as central to their experiences. Devon's story (Chapter 3) in particular demonstrates how friendships are important influences in newly emerging identities as their existing confident black identities and cultural wealth are challenged. The friendships of both boys and girls with children from similar cultural heritages may affirm their cultural identity, giving them confidence to challenge othering and marginalisation experienced through the domination of whiteness in the classroom. In addition, the close friendships with white peers, such as that of Devon and Alan, can support black children to understand new expectations of school norms whilst maintaining their primary black identities.

Identity and ethnicity – being black and British

Britishness can be correlated to whiteness as a dominant concept in the maintenance of British identity. As communities are othered in British society, cultural heritage is understood as being a primary indicator of identity despite families having long generational histories in Britain (Hirsch, 2018). It is important to clarify any confusion for children as they enter wider society by including the diversity of their cultural heritages within a single definition of Britishness. Ethnicity is socially constructed to distinguish groups in society. In racialised discourse, ethnicity is often used as an umbrella term to describe the other by unspoken exclusion of white people who may see themselves as separate and the unquestionable norm by which Britishness is defined. Ethnicity can be described as having particular cultural elements from birth through historical associations such as colonisation, with common sets of values, experiences and linguistic traits transmitted to generations through pride in heritage (Banks, 2001). It is often used as a term to categorise black people as a single homogenous group without recognition of unique cultures and experiences of racism. This denies how racism operates and may discriminate differently against marginalised groups within specific cultural heritages and historical contexts. If all children with a Caribbean heritage and culture are stereotyped as being of the same ethnicity, there is no acknowledgement of different languages and cultures across the different countries within the Caribbean basin. Many different ethnicities in the Caribbean contribute to cultural diversity being an important element in national identity in the region. These cultural signifiers are aspects of group identity for othered British communities through which they gain strength in adversity and comprise a cultural wealth on which to draw through united action (Yosso, 2005). This unity is particularly important to affirm a British identity that includes the diversity of cultures as historically contributing to a twenty-first century conception of being British. The cultural wealth of black British children should be recognised as essential when supporting the transition from home to school.

Categories used to differentiate between ethnicities of school populations for monitoring purposes can unintentionally exclude children from identifying with being British. Ethnic monitoring has been a non-statutory requirement for schools since 1990 but was not put to strategic use until the Stephen Lawrence enquiry (MacPherson, 1999). The report highlighted institutional racism as a cause for social unrest alongside data on black children's underachievement. Currently there remains no statutory duty to collect ethnic data, although this was strongly recommended to fulfil equality duties in the RRA Act 2000 to promote race equality and as a tool for compliance towards implementation of equality legislation. Ethnic monitoring has evolved in the current managerial ethos in education, primarily to promote educational outcomes by identifying underachieving children grouped by ethnicity. This is denoted through a focus on terms relating to cultural heritage rather than place of birth, such as black Caribbean, without affirmation that the children are primarily black British. Additional problems arise from collection of data in this way as the terms black and white used to identify ethnicity can result in national stereotypes by cultural and physical characteristics. Data can produce tensions between the need for information and homogenisation of groups of people through racialisation and biological definitions of 'race'. The categories used for monitoring contribute to marginalisation of national identity for young black children as they reinforce perceptions of whiteness as characteristic of Britishness. Both covert and overt references to officially not belonging to Britain at both managerial and interactional levels are examples of institutional racial microaggressions that can be reproduced through usually well-intentioned monitoring procedures.

What constitutes Britishness is relevant at the present time following the vote to leave the European Union that is polarising uneasiness regarding immigration and voiced as a perceived threat to British values and customs. Scapegoating across Europe and the USA portrays immigration as the cause of economic hardship and terrorism fuelled by rhetoric during periods of political upheaval. One result has been a rise in racist incidents to which black British children may be exposed personally as well as through media and community interactions. As discussed in the introduction, Britishness can be viewed out of a historical context of immigration as a fixed culture of whiteness superficially represented through notions such as 'fish and chips' being the national dish. The Prevent Strategy (HMG, 2011) may exacerbate this image of Britishness through requirements for all schools and early years settings to promote British values. Values can be interpreted as traditions rather than those beliefs that transcend cultures and religions. As part of the counterterrorism strategy, Prevent gives schools the duty to address any signs of radicalism in children, focusing on the Muslim community. This can stop parents communicating with practitioners about home life through concerns regarding false interpretations of their cultures and religions. One of the boys in the study, Jason, has a Muslim father but attends a Catholic school, the inherent religion of his mother. The practitioners were unaware that he attended the mosque each Friday as he did not mention this in class. He spent a morning playing in the construction area alone, representing the conflicting experiences of the Christian religion predominant in school and his identity as a Muslim. Without support, this conflict can contribute to confusion regarding his national identity, as the concept of Christianity is fundamental to populist perceptions of being British. The Prevent strategy can contribute to a sense of exclusion for Muslim children through disproportionate emphasis on terrorism in the Islamic community. It is important to understand, include and value children's cultural heritages within a common framework of Britishness. Chapter 8 discusses how children can be supported in early years environments through critical pedagogy that provides for expression and application of their cultural identities.

Summary

The denigration of race as a central element of identity formation may lead children to 'question their competence, intelligence and worth' (Delgado, 2000, p. 135). The consequences can begin as children start school, impacting on behaviour and motivation to learn. Assaults on identity through racial micro-aggressions can be a fundamental cause of disaffection with school that leads to underachievement and ultimately to exclusions. An understanding of the nuanced ways that micro-aggressions impact on identity can inform action to support children in forming positive identities of being black and British. A colour-blind approach, which attempts to treat all children the same for equality, negates the covert ways in which they are racialised through personal and institutional interactions during everyday activity. Black children have particular experiences of othering through marginalisation and racialisation of their identities that have been discussed as having both psychological and material impact on their education. The early years environment can be an exciting introduction to newly forming social relationships, but only when black children are supported by practitioners through awareness of how norms of whiteness can situate them as the other. As children become independent and enter new social worlds, opportunities to embrace the diversity of being British, including aspects of generational cultural practices, can give confidence to challenge racialisation. Peer friendships can support this transition alongside an inclusive environment that recognises their important contribution to curriculum delivery and the environment. The CRT precept of listening to voices of othered communities to understand and respond to experiences of racialisation can be an effective means towards the aim of providing positive, safe environments for early learning and development. The following three chapters tell the stories of black children to illustrate how everyday interactions contribute to their identity as both young learners and black British citizens.

Reflective practice

- Racial micro-aggressions have been discussed as psychologically damaging for the black child. How can you and others in the team become more aware of when they occur so as to be prepared, through both policy and practice, to support the children who experience them as well as to discuss reasons and consequences with those responsible for the micro-aggressions?
- Think of a situation when you have had to hide your personal identity in either a social or formal situation. How can you address a need for black children and their parents to mask their identities in the social world of the early years setting which may be dominated by white, middle-class cultural norms?
- What is your interpretation of colour-blindness? How do you think this impacts on your early years practice?

References

Askew, S. and Ross, C. (1998) *Boys Don't Cry-Boys and Sexism in Education*. Milton Keynes: Open University Press.

Baldock, P. (2011) *Understanding Cultural Diversity in the Early Years*. London: Sage Publications.

Banks, J. A. (2001) *Cultural Diversity and Education*. Boston, USA: Allyn and Bacon.

BBC (2005) *A Child of Our Time: Identity Crisis*. Available from www.bbc.co.uk/parenting. video/index.shtml. Accessed 22 July 2016.

Bradbury, A. (2013) *Understanding Early Years Inequality: Policy, Assessment and Young Children's Identities*. Oxon: Routledge.

Broadhead, P. and Burt, A. (2012) *Understanding Young Children's Learning through Play*. Oxon: Routledge.

Brooker, L. (2010) Learning to Play in a Cultural Context, in Broadhead, P., Howard, J. and Wood, E. (eds.), *Play and Learning in the Early Years*. London: Sage Publications.

Brown, B. (1998) *Unlearning Discrimination in the Early Years*. Staffordshire: Trentham Books.

Brown, B. (2001) *Combatting Discrimination*. Staffordshire: Trentham Books.

Brown, B. (2008) *Equality in Action: A Way Forward with Persona Dolls*. Staffordshire: Trentham Books.

Browne, N. (2004) *Gender Equity in the Early Years*. Berkshire: Open University Press.

Clark, R. and Clark, M. (1947) Racial Preference and Identification in Negro Children, in Newcomb, P. and Hartley, M. (eds.), *Readings in Social Psychology*. London: Holt.

Constantine, M. and Sue, D. W. (2007) Perceptions of Racial Micro-Aggressions among Black Supervisees in Cross-Racial Dyads, in *Journal of Counseling Psychology*, 54 (2) pp. 142–153.

Crenshaw, K. (1993) Whose Story Is It Anyway? Feminist and Antiracist Appropriations of Anita Hill, in Morrison, T. (ed.), *Race-ing Justice, En-Gendering Power*. London: Chatto and Windus.

Crenshaw, K. (1995) Intersections of Race and Gender, in Crenshaw, K., Gotanda, N., Peller, G. and Thomas, K. (eds.), *Critical Race Theory – The Key Writings That formed the Movement*. New York: The New Press.

Crenshaw, K. (2009) Mapping the Margins: Intersectionality, Identity Politics, and Violence against Women of Color, in Taylor, E., Gillborn, D. and Ladson-Billings, G. (eds.), *Foundations of Critical Race Theory in Education*. Oxon: Routledge.

Davis, K. (2007) *A Girl Like Me, Reel Works Teen Filmmaking*. Available from www.youtube. com. Accessed 22 July 2016.

Davis, P. C. (2000) Law as Microaggression, in Delgado, R. and Stefancic, J. (eds.), *Critical Race Theory: The Cutting Edge*. Philadelphia, USA: Temple University Press.

Delgado, R. (2000) Storytelling for Oppositionists and Others: A Plea for Narrative, in Delgado, R. and Stefancic, J. (eds.), *Critical Race Theory: The Cutting Edge*, 2nd ed. Philadelphia, USA: Temple University Press.

Dixson, A. and Rousseau, C. (2006) The First Day of School: A CRT Story, in Dixson, A. and Rousseau, C. (eds.), *Critical Race Theory in Education*. Oxon: Routledge.

Drury, R. (2007) *Young Bilingual Learners at Home and School: Researching Multilingual Voices*. Staffordshire: Trentham Books.

DuBois, W. E. B. (1994) *The Souls of Black Folk*. New York, USA: Dover Publications.

DuBois, W. E. B. (2009) The Conservation of Races, in Back, L. and Solomos, J. (eds.), *Theories of Race and Racism, a Reader*, 2nd ed. Oxon: Routledge.

Essed, P. (2013) Keynote Lecture: Everyday Racism and Resistance, in *Proceedings of the Racism and Anti-Racism through Education and Community Practice Conference*, June 26–28, 2013, Centre for Education for Racial Equality in Scotland: University of Edinburgh, Edinburgh, Scotland.

Fanon, F. (2008) *Black Skins, White Masks*. London: Pluto Press.

Graham, J. A., Cohen, R., Zbikowski, S. M. and Secrist, M. E. (1998) A Longitudinal Investigation of Race and Sex as Factors in Children's Classroom Friendship Choices, in *Child Study Journal*, 28 (4).

Harris, A. (2000) Race and Essentialism in Feminist Legal Theory, in Delgado, R. and Stefancic, J. (eds.), *Critical Race Theory: The Cutting Edge*, 2nd ed. Philadelphia, USA: Temple University Press.

Hart, I. (2009) *The Myth of Racist Kids*. London: Manifesto Club.

Her Majesty's Government (2011) *Prevent Strategy*. London: The Stationary Office.

Hirsch, A. (2018) *Brit(ish), on Race Identity and Belonging*. London: Jonathan Cape.

hooks, B. (1993) *Sisters of the Yam*. Boston, USA: South End Press.

Konstantoni, K. (2013) 'We're All Friends in Nursery': Moving beyond the Slogan and 'Safe' Approaches While Promoting Social Justice in Early Childhood, in *Proceedings of the Racism and Anti-Racism through Education and Community Practice Conference*, June

26–28, 2013, Centre for Education for Racial Equality in Scotland: University of Edinburgh, Edinburgh, Scotland.

MacNaughton, G. (2003) *Shaping Early Childhood*. Berkshire: Open University Press.

MacPherson, W. (1999) *The Stephen Lawrence Inquiry*. London: HMSO.

McGlothlin, H. E. (2004) *Children's Decision Making about Social Relationships: The Impact of Similarity, Racial Attitudes and Inter-Group Contact, University of Maryland*. Available from https://drum.11b.umd.edu/bitstream/1093/1489/1/umi-ums-1441.pdf. Accessed 1 August 2015.

Milner, D. (1975) *Children and Race*. London: Penguin.

Milner, D. (1983) *Children and Race: 10 Years on*. London: Ward Lock Education Co. Ltd.

Moody, J. (2001) Race, School Integration and Friendship Segregation in America, in *American Journal of Sociology*, 107 (3) pp. 679–716.

Robinson, K. and Jones Diaz, C. (2006) *Diversity and Difference in Early Childhood Education*. Berkshire: Open University Press.

Rollock, N., et al. (2015) *The Colour of Class*. Oxon: Routledge.

Sewell, T. (2010) Overcoming the 'Triple Quandary': How Black Students Navigate the Obstacles of Achievement, in Ochieng, B. M. N. and Hylton, C. L. A. (eds.), *Black Families in Britain as the Site of Struggle*. Manchester: Manchester University Press.

Sleeter, C. (2005) How White Teachers Construct Race, in Critchlow, W., Dimitriadis, G. and Dolby, N. (eds.), *Race, Identity and Representation in Education*. Oxon: Routledge.

Stone, M. (1981) *The Education of the Black Child in Britain*. Glasgow: Fontana.

Sue, D. W. (2010) *Microaggressions in Everyday Life*. Hoboken, New Jersey, USA: Wiley.

Van Ausdale, D. and Feagin, J. R. (2001) *The First R.: How Children Learn Race and Racism*. Lanham, Maryland, USA: Rowman and Littlefield.

Vaught, S. and Hernandez, G., et al. (2013) Post Racial Critical Race Praxis, in Lynn, M. and Dixson, D. (eds.), *The Handbook of Critical Race Theory in Education*. Oxon: Routledge.

Weiler, K. (2009) Feminist Analysis of Gender and Schooling, in Darder, A., Baltodano, M. and Torres, R. (eds.), *The Critical Pedagogy Reader*, 2nd ed. Oxon: Routledge.

Wilson, A. (1978) *The Developmental Psychology of the Black Child*. New York, USA: Africana Research Publications.

Winant, H. (2009) Race and Racism, in Back, L. and Solomos, J. (eds.), *Theories of Race and Racism, a Reader*, 2nd ed. Oxon: Routledge.

Wright, C. (1992) *Race Relations in the Primary School*. London: David Fulton.

Yosso, T. (2005) Whose Culture Has Capital? A Critical Race Theory Discussion of Community Cultural Wealth, in *Race, Ethnicity and Education*, 8 (1) pp. 69–91.

Zamudio, M., Russell, C., Rios, F. and Bridgeman, J. (eds.) (2011) *Critical Race Theory Matters: Education and Ideology*. Oxon: Routledge.

3

DEVON'S STORY – 'BEST FRIENDS'

The roles of friendships in the challenges to young black identities

Introduction

Devon's story tells of how friendships support him as he understands the culture of his reception class and uses his new knowledge to develop an emerging identity as black and British away from the security of his home environment. His story is told through a composite narrative depicting an afternoon of play in the forest area of the school grounds. Some of Devon's activities on a different occasion have been added to the narrative to emphasise how his friendships support him to maintain his strong black identity. Through collaboration with his white friend, Alan, he shares skills and knowledge acquired in the home to build a den, learning new techniques and using imagination to complete the construction. The two friends work together within expected boundaries of behaviour and independent activity. With his black friend, Neil, Devon is able to cross social and cultural boundaries between those of home and school. They do this through representations of their black identities and cultures to develop creativity and social relationships in the mainly white school culture. Devon's experiences reveal the conflict that many black children may have between his primary identity acquired from birth and a newly perceived racialised identity in the unfamiliar social world of school.

Devon's story

The reception class practitioners in Haremead School plan ongoing opportunities to make dens using a wide range of resources in both the indoor and outdoor classrooms. It is Tuesday morning and the class is timetabled for two hours of activity in the forest area, which consists of a network of paths winding through half an acre of bushes and trees in a corner of the extensive school grounds. The children are gathered in the central clearing. They sit on the grass listening to their teacher Ian suggesting ways to build a den using a wide range of natural materials and other props. He asks them to choose a partner to work with in pairs. Devon immediately calls out to his best friend Alan who agrees with a smile. As they stand up, Neil approaches Devon to be his partner but Alan and Devon ask him to go away. Ian hears them arguing and convinces them to form a threesome. Alan and Devon take three bamboo sticks and a roll of sticky tape from the pile of resources and carry the equipment up a path, followed by Neil. They find a spot where they begin to discuss the construction of their den. Alan goes back to the clearing, where he selects a metal-framed clothes drier to form a base for the den, while Devon and Neil pick up small sticks and use them as guns.

When Alan returns, they begin to work out how to fasten the poles and frame together. Some girls approach and they shout at them to '*go away*'. Neil leaves the group and bangs the bushes with a stick. Alan and Devon argue about how to fasten the poles. Alan walks away with the two poles, shouting out, '*I told you not to do that*'. Devon is still angry and tells Alan to '*Be by yourself then!*' to which Alan retorts that he will as he walks off ahead down the path. Devon and Neil follow him carrying the metal frame until they find a more isolated place away from other children. A boy, Fardis, and a girl, Sana, approach the group and Alan tells them to go away. Devon chases them waving a stick and hits Sana. He pokes Fardis in the face, making a small cut that bleeds slightly. Fardis spits at Devon, who shouts abuse at him as Neil joins him to chase Fardis and Sana out of sight. Alan ignores the conflict while he perseveres alone in joining the equipment with tape to make the den. As Devon returns, Fardis follows threatening him with a stick, saying, '*Shut up please*', which Devon ignores. Rosa, a practitioner, approaches, sees Neil climbing a tree and sends him to Ian. Fardis runs off screaming while Devon and Alan continue to join sticks. Devon comments on Fardis' reaction, stating, '*He's scared of everything*'. When Alan suggests that they should '*Tape him*', Devon objects emphatically, replying '*No!*' while handing Alan the tape. Alan takes it and runs after Fardis. Devon is now alone putting up the frame into a triangular shape.

When Alan returns they discuss the den as they work together. Alan suggests that they make his house with an attic. Devon does not reply but gets inside the triangle they have constructed, announcing, '*I'm trapped in jail*'. Alan asks if he should tape it more, but Devon says not to and suggests that they '*pretend we're trapped in jail in your house*'. They get inside together and Alan tapes the construction from inside while Devon sits down. Devon asks Alan if he can come to his house again, but Alan replies that he is '*not sure*'. It is a warm day and Alan asks Devon why he keeps his jacket on, asking if it is because '*it's cool*'. Devon agrees that is why he keeps it on and makes a movement with his shoulders common to rap artists in music videos. He sees Fardis approaching them and says, '*Oh my God he's coming!*' As Fardis joins them, Devon tries to discourage his involvement by shouting, '*We're trapped in jail*'.

Fardis walks off as Christina, another practitioner, arrives, asking if they would like some fabric to cover their den. Devon rejects her offer by saying, '*No, we're trapped in here. We're actually living here*'. Christina makes no further comment but leaves a piece of fabric on the ground as she walks away. Devon and Alan get out of the den and continue to tape it together from the outside. Fardis comes back and Devon picks up a stick, chasing him away while shouting, *'Kung Fu Ninja!'* Alan continues taping and Devon bangs the metal frame with a stick, pretending to hammer while they discuss the construction of the jail. Fardis returns and Devon states, *'You have biscuits!'* Fardis screams and seems threatened by Devon's comment. Devon reassures him by saying, *'I'm not getting you'*, as he leaves for the clearing to get a biscuit for himself. When he is gone, Fardis gets into the jail and holds it together, cooperating with Alan, who continues to tape it. Unpredictably, Fardis then smashes it to the ground and hides in the bushes as Devon returns with Neil, both eating biscuits while staring incredulously at the destroyed jail. Alan tells them, *'I've just done a brilliant thing and Fardis wrecked it. I wish you were here to hold it tight while I taped it'*. As Fardis comes out of the bushes Devon shouts, *'Fardis, you're not supposed to push it. You're a baby!'* Fardis walks off without reacting to the insult. Devon and Neil discuss how they can tie him up while they go into the bushes hitting them with sticks, leaving Alan alone with the frame. Devon returns to Alan, while Neil continues to play in the bushes. Devon suggests that they rebuild the jail and they support each other in the reconstruction.

After a while they successfully rebuild the jail and join Neil in the bushes. Neil hits Devon with a stick, causing him to cry loudly, attracting the attention of Christina, who intervenes. She tells them to make up and they hug each other. Neil calls Devon *'a baby'* to which Devon responds with the expletive *'F***ing!'* Christina shows her displeasure by replying sternly that, *'We don't use that word here!'* Devon asks, *'Why not? My Mum says that at home'*. Christina replies loudly, *'Well we don't say it in school!'* as she leaves them. Devon gets inside the frame and Neil approaches him saying that he is a *'baby'* because he cried. When Devon objects Neil agrees, commenting, *'OK you're not a baby. You're a big man'*. Alan joins the conversation by stating, *'Boys are big men, but Fardis is a baby'*. Devon adds, *'Girls are babies'*. The conversation then changes as they joke together about *'farting'* as Alan and Devon try to strengthen the frame with plastic joiners. Meanwhile Neil continues to hit the bushes with a stick. Devon gets into the completed jail and calls from inside, *'I'm shooting you!'* while pointing a stick at Neil.

Alan goes to get a biscuit, leaving Devon to improve the construction that has again come apart, while Neil is nearby playing in the bushes. Devon joins Neil and they pretend there is a lion in the undergrowth. Devon returns to the construction as he sees Alan coming back and the two friends resume their attempts to join the frame. As they work they discuss hunting the animal in the bushes and discuss whether it is a lion or a fox, moving from fantasy to possible reality. The conversation then turns back to role play and how they are going to trap people in their jail. Neil comes out of the bushes and begins to compose a rap with Devon as all three fasten the plastic joiners around the sticks. When they are satisfied their construction is secure, Devon gets inside the jail and Alan goes to get another biscuit, calling to Neil not to let Devon out. Neil thrashes around in the bushes with his stick as Devon sits in the jail quietly rapping. Sana approaches them and

Neil chases after her with the stick. When returning he tells Devon that he has '*hit her on the head with a stick*'. From within the jail Devon asks, '*Did she tell you off?*' referring to Christina. Neil replies in the negative and goes back into the bushes. Devon continues to rap while in jail until Alan returns and stands outside eating a biscuit. Devon begins a discussion with him about his family being in jail.

DEVON: *I wonder when my brother's going to come out of jail.*

ALAN: *Is he?*

DEVON: *Yes*

ALAN: *Is he going to school in jail?*

DEVON: *No he's arrested 'cos he's shot somebody. Actually, all of my family are trapped in jail. Only one isn't.*

ALAN: *Are they got in jail because they're lying and somebody else did it? What did they do?*

DEVON: *They shot somebody. Where's your biscuit? Is it in your tummy?*

He climbs out of the construction by lifting it up in the air.

DEVON: *I'm not trapped in jail. I'll take it all apart.*

Devon gets out of the jail while Alan fastens himself to a bush with the plastic joiners. Devon runs up to Alan calling out: '*I'm running away! I'm a prisoner and I have to run away from jail*'.

He goes back to the frame and gently kicks it, saying, '*Jail is stupid*'. As he crawls back in, the frame falls. He picks it up fondly, whispering, '*My little jail!*'

Ian then calls all the children back to the clearing as the session in the forest has ended. Neil runs off as Alan and Devon collect up all the resources and join the rest of the class sitting on the grass. Carl, who is sitting next to Devon, jokes by asking if he can marry him. Devon replies emphatically, '*Boys can't marry boys!*' They continue joking until Ian tells them to line up to go back to class as it is lunchtime. Walking back to the classroom, Ian notices the cut on Fardis' face and questions him about it. While the other children are in the classroom preparing to go to lunch, he unobtrusively ushers Alan, Devon and Neil out of the classroom with Fardis to discuss the incident.

Reflections on Devon's story

Factors influencing early friendship choices

Devon spends his time in the forest with both Alan and Neil but his first choice of partner is Alan, to whom he often refers as his 'best friend'. Devon has visited Alan's house once after school and when he asks if he can visit again, Alan replies that he is not sure. They come from differing home cultures and socio-economic groups, as Devon's parents are first-generation Jamaican and Sri Lankan; his mother is employed as a learning support assistant in a school and his father is a musician. Alan's heritage is white British, with both of his parents in professional employment. Parents can be influential in encouraging children's friendships, which are commonly representative of the culture and ethnicity of the family, although this does not seem to have influenced the special friendship between Devon and Alan. Parents often meet when their children start school and develop contacts through shared interests. This can initiate friendships between their children, who might then attend the same out-of-school activities. Patrick, Devon's father who was born in the Caribbean, was not observed speaking with Alan's parents before or after school despite Devon's visit to their home. Patrick rarely interacts with other parents, as Devon usually arrives as the bell rings to enter class. Another black parent informs him of events going on in the school, reflecting McGothlin's findings (2004) that same-race groups of parents interact in the playground. Alan's parents often speak to a group of four white parents who have similar cultural backgrounds. They are the parents of three boys in the reception class who Alan plays with when he is not playing with Devon alone or in a larger group of children, possibly indicating parental influence on friendship choices. On an occasion when Alan is absent from the group, his three white friends are together in the classroom at the Lego construction. Devon sits on the carpet next to them and attempts to join their play, but the group calls him names and tells him to go away in an attempt at exclusion. Devon resists the rejection by refusing to go, retaliating through reciprocal name-calling while sitting alongside them playing alone with the construction until the group leaves him.

McGlothlin (2004) found that 4-year-olds in early years settings typically interact with those who are like themselves, with white children accepting their own whiteness as the norm when discussing their in-group of friendships and only referencing skin colour when discussing peer out-groups. This same-race preference and racialisation of children's identities may not have been the primary reason for Devon's exclusion from the Lego activity. However, his personal awareness of skin colour as a signifier of difference can contribute to feelings of marginalisation in the mainly white school population. Devon's interpretation of his exclusion could also be partly influenced through more covert forms of racialisation, which can occur during everyday experiences both in and out of school. In contradiction, external factors that can influence friendships through intersections of race and class do not seem to have impacted on Devon and Alan's strong relationship as 'best friends'. Their friendship could be indirectly influencing Devon's acceptance by white peers when Alan is present in the group, as they then play together without conflict. Incidents of rejection and acceptance may contribute to a realisation for Devon of the dominant whiteness of the school culture. They may also reinforce his marginalisation in white peer group relationships as they seem to hold the power to decide on his inclusion.

Friendships to support early identities as black and British

A primary influence on Devon's early experiences in school is his racialised identity of being black and British. Friendships with white peers may be a means to understand and construct his British identity, a concept inextricably linked with whiteness in current discourse (see Chapter 2). Devon may construct personal meanings of whiteness in relation to his black British identity through the choice of a white peer as his best friend and their shared play experiences. This could be one reason why the other three boys in the study also develop close relationships with white boys, spending the majority of time with them during their daily class-room activity. Devon already has a strong positive Jamaican identity from home, as indicated in his occasional use of patois during play with Neil. In the classroom, he frequently speaks enthusiastically about his imminent visit to Jamaica in the summer holiday. Although often accepting of dominant preferences in society for the cultural whiteness of Britishness, when in school children are able to com-partmentalise other less acknowledged aspects of their identity and include them positively within a common British identity (McAdoo, 1985). For example, when asked about their nationality, children often give hyphenated responses such as British-Jamaican, indicating the strong relationship between the dual identity of family heritage and that of their place of birth.

Alan sees Devon as 'cool' when he refuses to take off his coat in the forest. Older white boys can envy black peers and see them as stylistically superior, choosing them as friends to identify with this desired image of black masculinity (Wright et al., 2000). Alan's comment indicates that he has internalised racialised stereo-types of black boys at an early age. The interaction reflects a particular notion of cool designated by Devon's blackness and clothes as signifiers of both race and masculinity that both boys seem to understand. Devon responds to their common notion of cool by making a shoulder movement associated with popular images portrayed in the media. By doing this he is possibly confirming his racialised identity through acceptance of stereotypes of black masculinity. The stylised cool image can mark belonging to a broader racialised group identity that gives strength to cope with and challenge experiences as an outsider within the school (Sewell, 2010). This cool image can contradict institutional expectations of dress codes in the school and may reaffirm negative stereotypes of black pupils as con-frontational and oppositional (Sewell, 1996). Positive aspects of blackness are often related to more populist notions of identity, such as styling of clothes alongside music, sport and dance abilities. As in Devon's case this can result in black children conforming to stereotypes to be accepted by white peers. For some children this can come at the expense of more positive, academic identities assigned to other racialised groups of children, influencing dispositions to learning and contribut-ing to underachievement in later stages in education (Milner IV, 2010).

Devon also has a strong relationship with Neil, with whom he spends much of his time when not with Alan. Neil is one of four black boys in the reception class. He also has a dual cultural identity as his father is black British with Jamaican heritage and his mother is Brazilian. The three boys are rarely observed playing together in the classroom or playground, which could make Ian's insistence of a threesome during the den play difficult for them. During informal discussions, practitioners refer to Neil as a troublesome child with special emotional needs although these have not been officially diagnosed and no specific classroom support has yet been identified. Young black boys are often seen as cute, although an unspoken fear of black youth is exacerbated through media representations and social discourse. This racialised stereotype results in a perceived need for control, beginning early in school when black children may begin to be seen as a problem, and this impedes an understanding of the unique difficulties they may have settling into the whiteness of the school (Ladson-Billings, 2011). Black parents give accounts of their young children being perceived in school as threatening and badly behaved, being punished with little evidence of these characteristics (Rollock et al., 2015). Black children can be considered disruptive when cultural stereotypes are assigned and institutional factors are not considered, such as conflicting cultural norms in school that may influence behaviour. This can lead to labelling of black children as troublesome, reproducing generalised stereotypes that may add to feelings of alienation in an environment in which they already feel culturally marginalised. Ian's decision to encourage the boys as a group of three in the forest is perhaps in recognition of Devon's existing relationships with both children and the benefits for Neil of working within the positive influences of Devon and Alan. He may also be responding to Devon and Neil's shared socio-cultural experiences that are beneficial to learning through play. Devon's decision to tell Alan to be by himself when they initially argue about their choice of resources could indicate a relationship dilemma, as he chooses to stay with Neil when Alan walks ahead. However, once they reform as a group of three, the importance of the task takes priority and they work cooperatively together. Engagement with a common goal can create opportunities for cooperation, as children are more likely to collaborate to problem-solve than engage in disruptive behaviour. Throughout the morning Neil uses both positive and negative strategies to divert Devon from the task-orientated, collaborative work with Alan. He does this successfully through the game of hunting animals, but intermittently uses language and actions not accepted in school to joke with Devon during their imaginative play. Devon's interactions with Neil indicate the importance of shared cultural meanings as a way of affirming their black identity in the school environment.

Cultural affirmation through friendships

Without adult intervention during the majority of time spent in the forest, Devon has the opportunity to express his cultural wealth with Neil, as the play allows them to communicate in patois. This brings together his experiences in the home and the school, although they can be perceived as inappropriate in the institutional environment. Acceptable cultural norms are reinforced through the hidden curriculum in imagery and practices, such as the use of language different to that in the home. This may be one reason why children in the study speak in dialect only when unheard by adults. They have understood that patois is considered unacceptable in the classroom but use it when possible to reaffirm their cultural identity and perhaps to challenge racialisation.

Music is important in Devon's life as he regularly accompanies his father to gigs and rehearsals. These experiences are reflected through frequent rapping and singing during play with Neil and Alan. Aspects of cultural wealth such as music are developed in black British communities partly to gain group strength in opposition to the oppression experienced through hegemonic racism (Patel and Tyrer, 2011). Black music is a crucial element of Devon's cultural wealth but can appear insignificant and not valued by omission from the mainstream curriculum. A conflict between the importance of genres of music heard in the home and marginalisation in the classroom can add to the cultural conflict experienced by young black children during their early days in school. Little provision is available for Devon's musical preferences, with weekly whole class music sessions restricted predominantly to traditional English songs. Lesson content is limited in comparison to the depth of quality, variety of genres and creative individuality available to Devon at home. His culture is devalued through the hidden curriculum as the emphasis on European music excludes relevance to his musical interests. Invalidation of black children's cultural experiences can contribute to negativity about school impacting on their identity as learners (Yosso, 2005). Reactions may be oppositional to expected norms of behaviour as children use their cultural wealth to oppose alienation and marginalisation in an environment of white cultural norms (Delgado, 2000). Devon and Neil have developed a relationship in which they can feel safe to challenge this conflict. Their defiance is indicated during play in the forest away from adults, where they represent their common experiences and reinforce their black identities. Lack of opportunities for cultural representations in the mainstream curriculum and ambiance of the setting may obviate practitioners' understanding of alternative contextual interpretations for black children's actions. Behavioural challenges resulting from feelings of marginalisation can be misinterpreted and may be read through a colour-blind lens that views whiteness as the normative standard. A colour-blind approach can deny and minimise the realities of race and racism, preventing alternative perspectives being acknowledged or valued (Constantine and Sue, 2007). Failure to recognise discriminatory institutional processes may exacerbate behavioural issues. Children may consider reprimands to be unreasonable, as reasons for rule breaking are either not understood or discussed between both parties, resulting in possible disaffection with school.

A conflict of cultural norms may lead to black children hiding their home experiences in the classroom, rendering them invisible in the predominance of whiteness (Bridgeman, 2011). Devon is inclined to hide expressions of his black cultural identity and is less reproved for his behaviour than is Neil, who is more overtly challenging. Their relationship may give Devon the confidence to express himself more freely through shared experiences such as interest in music as they rap confidently during their forest play when no adult can hear them. Opportunities afforded in the independent spaces available outside the watchful eyes of practitioners better allow for the emergence of children's cultural experiences to frame their learning and development (Broadhead and Burt, 2012). Devon indicates that he understands the consequences of not conforming to classroom norms when he uses headphones on a laptop to play rap music. On one occasion when he sees an adult approaching, the music video is quickly deleted in favour of a more acceptable educational programme. Acceptance of music as an important element of black children's cultural wealth is seen by Milner IV (2010, 2013) as essential when building a relationship with pupils within the white domain of the school. He finds that recognition of music as an expression of identity enables otherwise resistant children to respond more positively to learning through a culturally relevant classroom ethos and curriculum. A shared interest in music is also apparent in the relationship of Pina with her friend Remmie (Chapter 5) when they dance and sing to familiar music played regularly in the playground. In Frankfield School (Chapter 4) children's self-expression through rap, poetry and music are predominant in school assemblies to explore aspects of race and racism in society and ensure an inclusive curriculum relevant to black pupils. This acceptance of diverse music genres indicates awareness of the relevance to learning dispositions as children respond positively to representations of their home cultures.

Devon's story reveals how relationships with his two friends support him in different ways. His behaviour with Neil centres on fantasy play in the forest environment partly represented by elements of their cultural wealth. By contrast, when alone with Alan he mainly focuses on completion of the den as they develop a fantasy relevant to the set task of den building. Devon's close friendship with his best friend, who is familiar with the whiteness of the classroom ethos, may be one way in which he can understand and conform to the school norms. A means for Devon to develop coping strategies may be by forming relationships across racial and ethnic boundaries as an aspect of survival in the face of inconsistencies between white values in the school and those of his home and community (Sewell, 2010). Devon's interchangeable forest play between the more sustained and focused problem-solving activity with Alan and the cultural expressions applied to his activity with Neil can be viewed as an intuitive strategy for him to cope with cultural disparities. When Pina is faced with verbal micro-assaults in the playground regarding her hair, her relationship with Remmie gives her confidence to challenge the boy who racially abuses her (Chapter 5). Her friendship with another black child can be a support to feel psychologically safe to interact in the wider social context and face the challenge of racial micro-aggressions (Tatum, 1997). Commonality of experiences and sharing of cultural wealth can be important to challenge racism alongside a shared gendered and racialised identity. Devon's close relationships with both Neil and Alan help him to manage a possible double-consciousness to challenge the conflict between the institutional whiteness of school and cultural blackness of his home that influences his newly forming identity as black and British.

The early criminalisation of black boys

In the forest, Devon and Alan cooperate throughout to solve the challenge of joining the poles together in order to secure the frame for what becomes their jail, giving meaning to the task through imaginative play. They collaborate to develop their play, with Devon extending the imaginative element by introducing a story about his family being in jail. When Alan suggests that the den can be the attic in his house they compromise, using their shared experience of playing together at Alan's home and agreeing that the construction can be where they will live, as well as where they are trapped as prisoners. Opportunities offered to Devon and Alan for extended involvement in the role play allow them to express their realities within a realm of fantasy as they organise their understanding of the world (Bee-ley, 2014). Their mature strategy enables them to establish an affable relationship and engage in their activity for an extended period, absent of conflict. Construction play is temporarily halted when they concentrate on a discussion about Dev-on's family being in jail. Alan shows surprise, questioning the fact that they could have done wrong by asking Devon if someone lied about them, causing the family to be in jail. His incredulity indicates that either he has not internalised hegemonic stereotypes of black criminality, or alternatively he may not have related them to a racialised identity of his friend. The latter is reflective of an attitude which views characteristics of black people in personal relationships as different, while assign-ing stereotypes to homogenised, othered groups in society (Bonilla-Silva, 2010). Devon elaborates his story by saying that they shot somebody and then changes the subject to the more tangible one of the biscuits they have been eating. This is perhaps in recognition of Alan's concern, which may have meant further ques-tioning about the imaginative situation, thus nullifying the fantasy. Alternatively, he may not want to engage Alan further in the stereotype of criminalisation that could be personally internalised through interactions in his social world. The black community, including young children, can feel the need to hide their social realities when in a white, middle-class environment such as school. This can be due to awareness of deficit stereotypes of black communities through perceptions of aggression and law breaking as the cultural norm, as voiced in the stories of young black people involved in the Tottenham demonstrations (Fully Focused Community, 2014).

Devon's conversation with Alan could be misread as real if interpreted in the context of a historically racialised criminal justice system and institutionally rac-ist policing methods such as 'stop and search' (Glynn, 2013). The role play was discussed with Devon's father to better understand Devon's fantasy and dismiss any racialised notions that may influence the white researcher's interpretation. He was surprised at the idea of a family member in jail, as Devon has no brother or member of the family who is or has been sent to prison. He proposed that Devon may have overheard a topic of discussion in the family, as the trial in America of a Jamaican criminal and his deportation was an item in the British press at the time and discussed widely by the public and in the media. Children internalise racial understandings by listening to adult conversations and media representations that contribute to the development of their identity as black and British.

Misrepresentation of Jamaican culture through disproportionate exposure of negative events in the media can create racialised stereotypes of crime and violence. Through play children can represent their experiences at home and any contradictions of their cultures in the media. This may contribute to confusion in identity formation as negative stereotypes acquired from the dominant ideology might compound deficit models of black families that are not a reality in children's lives. These stereotypes relate to processes of criminalisation and may begin as early as when young children start school. Attitudes in society to the lawlessness of black youth are sometimes reproduced in the classroom and apparent in fear by practitioners of a lack of control (Ladson-Billings, 2011). Cultural stereotyping was observed in St. Zita school between Jason and his teacher, Angela, when during a phonics lesson she asks the class to name a word beginning with the sound 'Sh'. Jason calls out '*shoot*', which is frowned on by Angela, who replies that they do not like shooting in school. Jason immediately strongly objects by stating that he means '*a goal*'. Angela apologetically accepts his objection, later acknowledging to the researcher that her response was determined through either a lack of focus on sport or perhaps a racialised stereotype. Angela's reaction indicates the need for a critical pedagogy to question hierarchal preformed attitudes and provide opportunities for children to voice their perspectives on cultural misunderstandings.

Disobedience in school may also be attributed to a cultural stereotype of aggressive black boys rather than exploring alternative reasons. This can result in the administration of harsher and immediate punishment, causing resentment and further lack of conformity to school rules (Sewell, 1996). The stereotype of aggressive black boys can lead to a 'homogenous image of black masculinity' that is threatening to practitioners as it opposes the school ethos of non-violent behaviour (Wright et al., 2000, p. 75). An example of when black boys' acts of aggression could be mistakenly viewed through stereotyped notions is when Devon, Alan and Neil resist the attempts of Fardis to enter their play. Fardis is new to the class, having arrived recently in Britain with his family. He is not fluent in English and although wanting to join the play of the three boys, he has not yet learned the social conventions required for acceptance into the group. His strategy to join them is through verbal and physical aggression, to which the three boys similarly retaliate. The situation becomes out of control as there is no practitioner intervention and ends when Devon pokes him in the face with a stick, causing it to bleed. Fardis retaliates by spitting in his face, to which Devon verbally retaliates. When discussed with Patrick, Devon's father, he is shocked that someone in the class has been spitting. He justifies acceptable violence by placing meaning on Devon's response as a defensive reaction in retaliation to the physical and verbal racial micro-assaults from Fardis. This could reflect his racialising experiences, as he explains how he does not accept anyone spitting on him, indicating a possible response transmitted to Devon through sharing his own actions in opposition to incidents of racism.

When Ian, Devon's teacher, notices the cut on Fardis' face, he indicates an understanding of the effects of negative stereotyping by discussing the incident away from other children. This demonstrates an awareness of the consequences of reprimanding the boys in front of their peers, which could reinforce the stereotype of violent black masculinity to the rest of the class. If constantly reprimanded in front of the class, black children can adopt a stereotyped identity as the 'bad' boy or girl, which then determines their learner identity in the peer group (Ladson-Billings, 2011). As well as avoiding this stereotype, withdrawal from the classroom gives space to better understand why Devon acted in this way rather than through unquestionable interpretation of their actions as rule breaking used to challenge classroom norms. Time for discussion with the children involved can allow for constructive challenge to dominant power relations in the classroom with adults and peers whereas racialised assumptions contribute to marginalisation and alienation of black children (Giroux, 2009). This approach promotes awareness of reasons for children's behaviour rather than habitually promoting conformity to school expectations. Practitioners may feel that they are immune from racial assumptions in wider society in the common aim towards an inclusive learning environment (Zamudio et al., 2011). Consequently, they could deny not only their own attitudes, but also those of children by isolating experiences of racism from the classroom environment as a means to create an ethos of equality. However, equality through denial of racism is not a reality as children's internalisation of racialised experiences cannot be ignored. Ian's response to the conflict recognises the importance of affording time and private space for the boys to give their personal perspectives on the situation while reasserting rules for unacceptable behaviour. He critically discusses their behaviour with them instead of acting judgementally from his position of power in the classroom and through any preformed assumptions.

Intersections of race and gender in friendships

CRT focus on the centralisation of race and intersections with other aspects of identity such as gender allows for interpretation of important influences on friendship choices. All children in the study had close same-gender friendships, which has been suggested as more important than same race in determining close relationships (Graham et al., 1998). Close friendships between Devon, Sonic and Louis with white boys contradict research evidence that black children's friendships are predominantly same race, as all three boys had very special best friend relationships with white boys (Moody, 2001; Shritts et al., 2013). However, McGlothlin (2004) found that boys have more cross-raced friendships than girls. She suggests this is mainly because boys base their friendships on common interests rather than cultural similarities, such as the superhero play in Sonic's story (Chapter 4). Sonic indicates the importance of their common interest by choosing their pseudonyms based on the interactive game regularly played with his best friend at home and in school. Devon's friendship with Alan does not focus on any particular interest, but rather on their collaborative relationship, whereas the relationship between two other boys in the project demonstrates alternative reasons for their close friendships. Louis attends Gasgoyne School with his best friend, Lewis, who is white. There are no other children with the same African-Caribbean cultural background as Louis in the class. Lewis is often absent and when Louis is aware that his friend is not coming, he is sad at first and then either contentedly plays alone or seeks adult attention to support his activity. When engaged in groups of children without Lewis, Louis often ends up in conflict situations. His relationship with his white friend seems to give him a sense of security and confidence to interact more easily with others in the classroom. Martino and Pallotta-Chiarolli (2003) offer a view that black boys' dependence on close relationships is used as a blanket of security against negative stereotypes of black males that exist in schools. They suggest that black girls do not always feel so threatened in the classroom context and therefore have less need for close relationships. Some evidence of this is the friendships of Kylie and Shania who attend two different schools in this study. Neither girl appears to have special friendships but interact with their peers according to the context of their chosen activity. They are confident to follow their interests either alone or playing with varying groups of children. For example, Kylie (Chapter 4) referees a football match played by up to seven boys for twenty minutes. Shania confidently leads play with a group of six children, for the full fifteen minutes of morning break in the school garden, as they 'dig the way to Australia'. Neither girl indicates dependency on close relationships with peers but can confidently take the lead in large groups. Only Pina (Chapter 5) has a special friend in the classroom from whom she is inseparable. Pina's 'best friend', Mariam, comes from a different, though still othered, Sri Lankan heritage. They have no particular interest that they both follow, but engage cooperatively in a range of activities both in the classroom and outside during playtimes. It could be argued that Pina seeks support for her experiences of racialisation by developing an additional relationship in the playground with Remmie, who has a similar African-Caribbean heritage. This suggests the importance to her of a commonality of identity in friendships, as seen in the relationship of Devon with his black friend Neil.

During forest play, Neil calls Devon 'a baby' for crying, to which Devon retaliates through a masculine stereotype of swearing. Devon, Alex and Neil state that only girls can be called babies and that boys are 'big men', reinforcing a macho stereotype of males not showing their emotions. The group also call Fardis a baby, thus insulting his masculinity for reactions to being chased away from their area in the forest. Although this macho aspect is assigned to male identity generally, Howard and Reynolds (2013, p. 238) suggest that black males are narrowly identified in schools through a 'hyper masculine construct' and are excluded from peer groups if they do not comply with these norms. This racialised and gendered stereotype is affirmed by the boys in their comments despite contrary evidence from the emotional reactions of both Fardis and Devon. Devon and Neil show solidarity towards hyper-masculinity through disdain for the two women present in the classroom who are not in authority, the researcher and a school student on work experience placement. On two occasions they whisper abuse together and loudly call the women names such as 'smelly pants' while giggling. Connolly (2009) suggests use of sexualised, gendered behaviour by black boys in reception classes can be seen to assert racialised perceptions of masculine identity while forming new relationships as they begin school. Devon's understanding of his gendered identity is indicated through general peer group interactions, as he was not observed playing with girls either in groups or with individuals throughout the research period. During forest play Neil scares Sana away from the den construction by shouting for her to '*go away*' on two occasions and eventually hitting her with a stick. Devon shows concern related to his understanding of appropriate school behaviour by asking Neil if he was '*told off*' by the practitioner. However, on four separate occasions in the playground Devon uses his masculinity to torment girls with threats that go unchallenged but have the effect of excluding them from the play situation. On a separate occasion, Devon reacts emotionally to comments regarding his plaited hairstyle, as he may perceive this as a threat to his gendered identity. These situations indicate that Devon and Neil have already understood how generally applied stereotypes of masculinity are exaggerated when assigned to black boys. Perhaps they adopt these negative racialised stereotypes to assert their black male identity but in a way that can be detrimental to their future dispositions to school.

Summary

Devon's story demonstrates how friendships are an important element in children's newly emerging identities as they give support to maintain the formative, confident black identities from home through aspects of shared cultural wealth. Friendships of both boys and girls with children from similar cultural heritages can affirm their cultural identity. This gives them confidence to challenge othering and exclusion experienced through the hierarchy of whiteness in the classroom. Devon's story indicates how important it is to understand and take action to minimise exposure to and reproduction of false, negative perceptions of black male identity. By offering support for alternative positive learner identities and building on the realities of children's individuality, the adoption of racialised stereotypes of black male identity can be challenged. This should be in conjunction with action against the hidden curriculum of institutional processes and practices that reproduce stereotypes and marginalise black children. Close friendships with white peers, such as that of Devon and Alan, enable the four black boys in the study to adapt to norms of whiteness through developing a double-consciousness that facilitates access to educational experiences. The three girls in the study are less dependent on relationships with white peers or special friendships to conform to classroom expectations and use their individualism to challenge stereotyping and marginalisation while accessing support when required. The following chapter tells how play can afford opportunities for children to develop friendships and represent their identities through independent activity.

Reflective practice

- Observe close relationships between children in your setting to understand how gendered and racialised identities are important in these friendships.

- How are hierarchical relationships determined in group play situations and what strategies are used to determine and maintain roles?
- How do children in your setting affirm their cultural identity with both peers and adults? Are the interactions positive or do they sometimes reflect cultural stereotypes, and why may this be?

References

Beeley, K. (2014) *Creative Role-Play in the Early Years*. London: A&C Black.

Bonilla-Silva, E. (2010) *Racism without Racists*. Lanham, Maryland, USA: Rowman and Littlefield.

Bridgeman, J. (2011) African American Counter Narratives, in Zamudio, M., Russell, C., Rios, F. and Bridgeman, J. (eds.), *Critical Race Theory Matters: Education and Ideology*. Oxon: Routledge.

Broadhead, P. and Burt, A. (2012) *Understanding Young Children's Learning through Play*. Oxon: Routledge.

Connolly, P. (2002) *Too Young to Notice, the Cultural and Political Awareness of Three to Six Year Olds in Northern Ireland*. Northern Ireland: Bellair Community Relations Information Centre.

Constantine, M. and Sue, D. W. (2007) Perceptions of Racial Micro-Aggressions among Black Supervisees in Cross-Racial Dyads, in *Journal of Counseling Psychology*, 54 (2) pp. 142–153.

Delgado, R. (2000) Storytelling for Oppositionists and Others: A Plea for Narrative, in Delgado, R. and Stefancic, J. (eds.), *Critical Race Theory: The Cutting Edge*, 2nd ed. Philadelphia, USA: Temple University Press.

Fully Focused Community (2014) Riot from Wrong, in *Proceeding of Conference 'Thinking Spaces'*, June 19, 2014, The Tavistock and Portman NHS Foundation Trust: Tavistock Centre, London.

Giroux, H. A. (2009) Teacher Education and Democratic Schooling, in Darder, A., Baltodano, M. and Torres, R. (eds.), *The Critical Pedagogy Reader*. Oxon: Routledge.

Glynn, M. (2013) *Black Men, Invisibility and Crime-Toward a Critical Race Theory of Desistance*. Oxon: Routledge.

Graham, J. A., Cohen, R., Zbikowski, S. M. and Secrist, M. E. (1998) A Longitudinal Investigation of Race and Sex as Factors in Children's Classroom Friendship Choices, in *Child Study Journal*, 28 (4).

Howard, T. C. and Reynolds, R. (2013) Examining Black Male Identity, in Lynn, M. and Dixson, A. D. (eds.), *Handbook of Critical Race Theory in Education*. Oxon: Routledge.

Ladson-Billings, G. (2011) Boyz to Men? Teaching to Restore Black Boys' Childhood, in *Race Ethnicity and Education*, 14 (10) pp. 7–15.

Martino, W. and Pallotta-Chiarolli, P. (2003) *So What's a Boy: Addressing Issues of Masculinity and Schooling*. Maidenhead: Oxford University Press.

McAdoo, H. (1985) Racial Attitude and Self-Concept of Young Black Children over Time, in McAdoo, H. and McAdoo, J. (eds.), *Black Children: Social, Educational and Parental Environments*. London: Sage Publications.

McGlothlin, H. E. (2004) *Children's Decision Making about Social Relationships: The Impact of Similarity, Racial Attitudes and Inter-Group Contact*. University of Maryland. Available from https://drum.11b.umd.edu/bitstream/1093/1489/1/umi-ums-1441.pdf. Accessed 1 August 2015.

Milner IV, H. R. (2010) *Start Where You Are, But Don't Stay There*. Cambridge, MA, USA: Harvard University Press.

Milner IV, H. R. (2013) Analyzing Poverty, Learning, and Teaching through a Critical Race Theory Lens, in *Review of Research in Education*, 37 (March) pp. 1–53. Available from http://rre.aera.net. Accessed 9 July 2017.

Moody, J. (2001) Race, School Integration and Friendship Segregation in America, in *American Journal of Sociology*, 107 (3) pp. 679–716.

Patel, T. and Tyrer, D. (2011) *Race, Crime and Resistance*. London: Sage Publications.

Rollock, N., et al. (2015) *The Colour of Class*. Oxon: Routledge.

Sewell, T. (1996) *Black Masculinities and Schooling: How Black Boys Survive Modern Schooling*. Staffordshire: Trentham Books.

Sewell, T. (2010) Overcoming the 'Triple Quandary': How Black Students Navigate the Obstacles of Achievement, in Ochieng, B. M. N. and Hylton, C. L. A. (eds.), *Black Families in Britain as the Site of Struggle*. Manchester: Manchester University Press.

Shritts, K., Pemberton, C., Roben, K. and Spelke, E. (2013) Children's Use of Social Categories in Thinking about People and Social Relationships, in *Journal of Cognition and Development*, 14 (1) pp. 35–62.

Tatum, B. (1997) *Why Are All the Black Kids Sitting Together in the Cafeteria?* New York, USA: Basic Books.

Wright, C., Weekes, D. and McGlaughlin, A. (2000) *'Race', Class and Gender in Exclusions from School*. London: Falmer Press.

Yosso, T. (2005) Whose Culture Has Capital? A Critical Race Theory Discussion of Community Cultural Wealth, in *Race, Ethnicity and Education*, 8 (1) pp. 69–91.

Zamudio, M., Russell, C., Rios, F. and Bridgeman, J. (eds.) (2011) *Critical Race Theory Matters: Education and Ideology*. Oxon: Routledge.

4

KYLIE'S AND SONIC'S STORY – 'CAN WE PLAY NOW?'

Early years pedagogy and black children's education

Introduction

The key focus for this chapter is how pedagogies can impact on black children's early years education. Kylie's and Sonic's experiences are framed through a pedagogy led by the curriculum guidance for the Early Years Foundation Stage. Play has been a dominant approach in early years education as it allows children to explore concepts in pace with their individual developmental levels and previous experiences. The concept of school readiness has recently become a government priority in education and has resulted in an aim for young children to attain in the more academic subjects (McDowall Clark, 2017). The EYFS curriculum is now primarily aimed at preparing children for the next stage in education. Settings are accountable through inspections that require accountability measured by developmental objectives. Pressure for school readiness places additional stress on practitioners for ensuring outcomes in the *Early Years Foundation Stage Profile* (DfE, 2017a) are met by all children by regardless of their individuality. Accountability for meeting and recording curriculum planning and children's achievements results in a managerial culture pervading the classroom. The ensuing formalised pedagogy reduces time for critical reflection and engagement with the specific needs of children. A managerial role can be described as one of a technician who delivers prescribed outcomes rather than a more reflexive role that considers practice in relation to wider cultural implications (Rowan and Honan, 2005). This tends to position practitioners rather than enable them to position themselves critically to reflect on the developmental needs of the child (Kingdon, 2014). These demands have resulted in playful pedagogies implemented to balance accountability with opportunities for children to enhance their learning through experiences that support conceptual understandings.

Sonic and Kylie attend separate reception classes in Frankfield School. There are a majority of black children in both classes. Kylie is first-generation British as her mother and father were both born in Jamaica. Sonic is second-generation with Nigerian and Jamaican heritage. Although events informing their story are factual, the children and practitioners are located in one classroom for the purpose of this composite narrative. As the reception team plan jointly for the term's teaching, both children's classes are similar in relation to curriculum delivery and organisation of the environment within daily routines. Observations of Kylie and Sonic have been condensed into one morning to consolidate events and include as much of the data as possible to represent their learning experiences in the narrative. The routine is representative of the daily timetable with minor adaptations, such as weekly sessions in the computer suite rather than in assembly. Kylie's and Sonic's morning consists of extended periods of practitioner-led teaching using the whiteboard. These periods of whole class teaching alternate with periods of self-directed activity in the areas resourced for play. A balance between a curriculum-led pedagogy and playful pedagogy is recommended as good-quality practice in the report *Effective Provision of Pre-school Education* (EPPE) (Sylva et al., 2004) and is common practice in many reception classrooms. The recommendations can result in conflict for practitioners as compromises are made between pedagogic styles of learning through self-directed activity and more formal instruction. Practitioners in Frankfield manage this conflict by organising a timetable to meet assessment requirements to monitor achievement both internally by school management and externally through annual electronic data submitted to the local authority. This has resulted in shorter periods being available for child-initiated activity as priority is given to support for meeting planned objectives through predetermined activities. Allocation of time in the daily routines of reception classes for practitioner-led group teaching has increased significantly in the Early Years Foundation Stage (EYFS) since initial introduction of the assessment requirements in the Foundation Stage Profile (QCA, 2003; DfE, 2017a). These demands have resulted in limited opportunities for self-directed learning in the more freely resourced areas of the reception class environment. Less time for learning through playful activity restricts opportunities for Kylie and Sonic to express their socio-cultural experiences and is discussed here as marginalising their home cultures and identities. The development of early years policy has been from a laissez-faire approach based on individual child development to one of curriculum standardisation and accountability. When viewed at a macro political level, policy shift in early years education can be understood as a tool to maintain social hierarchies (Lea, 2014). In the context of black children's experiences of marginalisation this could be interpreted as also maintaining dominance of whiteness in education. Kylie's and Sonic's counter-narrative tells of how they use strategies to circumvent marginalisation to gain access to the curriculum.

Kylie's and Sonic's story

It is Friday morning in Kylie's and Sonic's reception class. The majority of space in the classroom is filled with tables and chairs for children to participate in adult-planned and directed activities. Spaces surrounding the tables are aimed at resourcing areas of learning in the EYFS curriculum (DfE, 2017b). These include literacy, mathematics, understanding the world, and creativity through imaginative play. Children are selected by practitioners to play in these spaces for short periods, which are timetabled alongside the more adult-directed activities. The area aimed at promoting mathematics is resourced with construction blocks placed on the carpet close to other resources such as puzzles, accessible to the children on shelving units. The imaginative play area is currently a hospital that includes office resources such as a telephone and clipboards with paper and pencils to support language and early writing skills. In a corner of the room, the permanent literacy area is set out with mark-making resources and books displayed on a shelf nearby, with brightly coloured cushions encouraging children to relax while reading. There is no creative art area in the classroom, as this is usually provided outside in the playground, shared by nursery and reception classes. As it is cold and damp on this day, the outside area is not set out for play.

Before the children arrive, Mrs. Paterson, the nursery nurse, is preparing for the main activity, which is to make Diwali lamps as the school is celebrating the Hindu festival. She places clay, glitter and paint on the table with her model of a lamp for the children to use as inspiration. She refers to her list of children's names to determine who has completed a lamp and comments, *'Just these three and I'm done'*. There is a large carpeted area where children sit for group sessions during the majority of the day. Mrs. Pandita, the teacher, is preparing the morning literacy lesson on the whiteboard. They discuss the routine of the coming school day and children's activity from the previous day, consulting their curriculum charts for planned activities and teaching objectives, as they busily prepare the classroom.

It is nine o'clock and Mrs. Paterson opens the classroom door for the children to enter. Having said goodbye to her mother, Kylie runs up to Mrs. Paterson, smiling, and gives her a hug. Mrs. Paterson helps take off her coat, which Kylie hangs on her peg. Sonic is one of the last to enter the classroom and laughs animatedly with his friend Mario as the children sit down on the carpeted area. After five minutes, the door is closed and Mrs. Paterson sits on a small chair at the edge of the group while Mrs. Pandita sits facing the children for registration. This morning the children are answering to their names in French, which is taught once a week to the class by a specialist teacher. Sonic answers loudly, *'Bonjour'*, while Kylie just smiles. Mrs. Pandita encourages her to answer by saying that she can answer in German or Italian if she prefers. Kylie continues to refuse to do so. Mrs. Pandita says jokingly that she will have to mark her as absent. Kylie looks down as some of the class laugh. At the end of registration the children are asked to line up by the door for assembly. She calls the boys first, who stand in line by the door, followed by the girls.

The thirty children walk into the large hall and sit nearest to the stage. Two rows of chairs are at the back of the hall for parents who have been invited to this special assembly, as Year 5 are performing the story of Rama and Sita to celebrate Diwali. Mrs. Edwards, the head teacher, begins by welcoming the parents who represent the racial and ethnic diversity of the school community. She emphasises the importance of the whole community participating in the range of religious celebrations and festivals of pupils, saying how pleased she is that so many parents have attended. She then introduces children in Year 5 who perform the story on the stage. Kylie and Sonic sit quietly, cross-legged, with the rest of their class throughout the twenty-minute performance. When it ends, they are attentive to Mrs. Edwards as she talks about the importance of respecting each other's religions and customs and that despite obstacles in life all children have equal rights to education and must strive to achieve. She gives information to parents on the following week's assembly, inviting them to attend. Mrs. Edwards then asks everyone to stand up and shake the hand of the person next to them and say 'I respect you', which is the custom at the end of special weekly assemblies. Kylie stands but does not shake hands or repeat the slogan while Sonic roughly shakes Mario's hand up and down, laughing with him. The reception class is the first to leave the hall.

The children enter the classroom and sit on the carpet where Mrs. Pandita is preparing the whiteboard for the whole-class phonics lesson. Mrs. Paterson distributes whiteboards, markers and cloths and then sits on a low chair on the edge of the group. Kylie shifts along the carpet to sit next to Mrs. Paterson and strokes her leg. Sonic sits at the back of the group next to Mario and they smile together as they settle down cross-legged. Mrs. Pandita gains the children's attention by pointing out the alphabet letters on the whiteboard. Children sound the letters in unison as she points to them. Sonic answers all correctly, smiling and laughing with Mario. He sits still while writing words from the whiteboard following Mrs. Pandita's instructions. Sonic raises his hand to each question, persevering until he is praised when correctly reading the word 'snap'. He yawns but remains attentive, ignoring children around him who are fidgeting and becoming distracted. Kylie participates in the lesson by sounding the words and attempting to write the sentences on her individual whiteboard. She also yawns but loses concentration looking up at Mrs. Paterson, who encourages her to continue. Kylie completes writing the sentence 'Nip is in the tin' and then pushes Abi, who is leaning on her. She appeals to Mrs. Paterson, who tells Abi to stop annoying Kylie. Meanwhile Sonic is praised for the second time as he correctly answers 'full stop' to Mrs. Pandita's next question. He smiles and looks happily at Mario.

The whiteboards are collected and children are asked to put on their coats and line up at the door in readiness to go outside. The children go into the larger Infant playground with Mrs. Paterson to 'run around', as the EYFS playground is not in use due to inclement weather. While children watch, Mrs. Paterson makes a kite out of a large plastic bin bag with a ball of wool to hold it by. She flies the kite by running up and down the playground with children coming and going from the group. Kylie stays close to her throughout as they all discuss why the kite is staying in the air. She takes a turn to hold the kite, trying to keep it in the air as they run. After her turn she sits refereeing a group of boys who are playing football. Sonic is initially interested in the kite-flying but shortly breaks out of the group with six other boys to play a superhero imaginative game, which is sustained until the end of the outdoor session. Their game is resourced through a large plastic map of Britain attached to a brick wall. Their fantasy centres on escaping from the Loch Ness Monster pictured on the map and they choose a home base on the map for each superhero, which they then represent individually in areas of the playground. The group applies their various home dialects to expressions of excitement and other emotions as they run to and from their home bases fleeing from the imaginary monster and helping each other escape to return safely '*home*'.

After twenty minutes of activity the children return to the classroom, where they take off their coats and sit on the carpet. Kylie takes Mrs. Paterson's hand, who asks if she had a cuddle at home today. Kylie replies negatively and sits next to her hugging her leg. When another girl, Naomi, cuddles the other leg, Kylie tries to push her off and, when unsuccessful, sobs quietly. Mrs. Paterson speaks softly to her, detaching both children from her legs. Kylie then stops crying and listens to Mrs. Pandita as she tells the three children who have not made Diwali lamps to go to the table with Mrs. Paterson. Kylie asks to join them and, although she has already made a lamp, it is agreed that she can make a second one as there is space at the table. She and the other children talk to Mrs. Paterson about their models as they work.

Meanwhile, the rest of the class is instructed in a mathematics lesson on number. Whiteboards and markers are allocated to the children, who watch as Mrs. Pandita writes a number line from one to ten on the interactive board. Sonic names the numerals as Mrs. Pandita points to them, contributing to the lesson throughout. He writes '2' on his board in response to the question, '*One less than three?*' He smiles when told his answer is correct. When Kylie finishes making her lamp she collects a whiteboard and marker and joins the class on the carpet. Mrs. Pandita rubs out the sums she has written and then continues the lesson by asking individual children to write addition sums on the board. Sonic eagerly puts up his hand to contribute but is not asked. The lesson continues with Mrs. Pandita writing three more sums on the board, while the children guess the answers and copy the sums on their individual whiteboards. Kylie does not attempt to do this and uses the board to make patterns similar to those on the Diwali lamps. Sonic writes accurate sums on his board and puts his hand up, unsuccessfully attempting to contribute to the lesson. Mrs. Pandita impatiently and frequently tells him to put his hand down, which he ignores, continuing to raise his hand at each question.

The lesson ends, boards are collected and the children are able to use the resources in the classroom for fifteen minutes to choose their activities. Some children read individually with Mrs. Paterson while Mrs. Pandita sits at the interactive board supporting children with a numeracy game. Kylie discusses the African snails with a group of four girls. They are in a tank placed near to Mrs. Paterson, at whom Kylie periodically glances as she is sitting nearby. After a few minutes, Mrs. Paterson chooses Kylie to read. Meanwhile, Sonic sits at the Mobilo construction with Mario and a group of four other boys making a long 'truck'. He proudly shows his construction to Mrs. Pandita, who is still at the interactive board. She asks him how many wheels it has and he replies '*four*'. He discusses this with Mrs.

Pandita as she briefly helps him to understand that there are four each side, making eight in total, until she is distracted by other children directing her focus back to the whiteboard numeracy activity. Sonic does not fully understand the concept of addition in relation to the positions of wheels on the vehicle, as his conclusion is that he will '*add another one*'. Instead, he stands watching the children at the interactive board until it is time to tidy the resources away and prepare for lunch.

Reflections on Sonic's and Kylie's story

Pedagogy and the relevance to black children's experiences

Much of Sonic's and Kylie's morning is spent in a large group, either in assembly or formal lessons. This is typical of their daily routine, which may include other forms of instruction such as physical exercise and language tuition. For young children, an over-formalised pedagogy can restrict learning by creating high anxiety levels and low self-esteem (Siraj-Blatchford and Siraj-Blatchford, 2007). Children find ways to cope with and challenge these feelings through negotiation of situations that may initiate stress by not conforming to expectations of the classroom culture. Such strategies can go unnoticed or be misinterpreted as deliberately uncooperative or defying norms of behaviour. Kylie may be exhibiting stress when she resists classroom routines, such as not answering when names are called in registration and not shaking hands as expected at the end of the assembly. Kylie finds it difficult during group sessions to concentrate on the learning objectives. She seeks Mrs. Paterson's attention by sitting next to her and stroking her leg, possibly to reduce the anxiety induced by that situation. The differing behaviours of Kylie and Sonic contradict common stereotypes of black boys having to be physically active learners with girls more able to concentrate during activities for longer periods. Sonic finds it less stressful than Kylie in the group teaching situations. He concentrates, sitting cross-legged as expected, throughout the session while continuously attempting to contribute. This could reveal that the more formal pedagogy better suits his learning style. Sonic maintains concentration as he participates throughout the lesson, ignoring children in the group who fidget and distract each other. His disposition to learning counters generalised stereotypes and indicates the importance of addressing institutional and structural factors that can racialise groups of children. When categorising children within these frameworks it is common to assign racialised gender designations to black girls and boys as groups of learners rather than critically reviewing the appropriateness of teaching methods or curriculum content (Bradbury, 2013). If children are not challenged intellectually through appropriate teaching methods they can become stereotyped as 'bad' children in the class although their actions may be to alleviate boredom or stress.

Although children need appropriate discipline, account should be taken of their different learning styles and cognitive abilities to provide an inclusive pedagogy, preventing racial stereotypes. Wright et al. (2000) suggest that black girls can feel it is easier to conform to classroom norms in recognition of their powerlessness to make changes within the hierarchies of whiteness and teacher/pupil relationships. Black boys tend to argue and challenge authority, acting out what could be perceived as stereotypical confrontational masculine identities (Sewell, 1996). In contrast, black girls are seen as good pupils when their resistance to racism and sexism in education is through negotiation and non-confrontational means. Individual accommodations to the norms of the classroom, such as compliance during group sessions, contribute to a positive gendered learner identity. Despite these stereotypical modes of behaviour, Kylie is the one to defy classroom expectations, while Sonic enjoys group instruction, participating within the boundaries of accepted behaviour while others around him lose concentration. Kylie and Sonic demonstrate how young children use their agency in the constitution of learner identity, contradicting commonly perceived racialised and gendered norms.

Using agency to access opportunities for learning

Kylie and Sonic have established very different relationships with the practitioners. Sonic has few personal interactions with either Mrs. Pandita or Mrs. Paterson. He spends more time with his peers, approaching adults only when he needs specific support for his activity or when in occasional disputes with peers. In contrast, Kylie spends her time in either direct contact or close proximity to Mrs. Paterson throughout the morning. The relationship between Kylie and Mrs. Paterson is encouraged as it is assessed to be important for her emotional development. An alternative perspective could be that she is conforming to a gendered stereotype of girls' need for affection to gain attention from Mrs. Paterson to support her learning, as class size and other managerial demands can make it difficult for practitioners to give individual attention. Kylie's show of affection towards Mrs. Paterson may be a partial strategy to develop their relationship as a response to an understanding of expectations of being 'good pupils' and therefore getting attention through positive interactions, thus gaining particular advantages. Kylie's relationship enables her to opt out of the structured group session in order to make a second Diwali lamp, where she accesses individual cognitive support during the activity that is not possible in the whole group teaching sessions where she loses concentration. When participating in whole group sessions Kylie maintains a close physical presence to Mrs. Paterson, who gives support for her social relationships and concentration on the lesson. She also ensures that she gets attention to her reading skills by staying close to Mrs. Paterson as children are called individually to read. Kylie frequently makes eye contact with her while standing nearby with a group of girls discussing the snails. Her behaviour supports the view that black girls adopt a range of strategies to interact with practitioners to challenge marginalisation rather than through more confrontational ways commonly used by black boys (Wright et al., 2006). Kylie is seen as a good pupil despite Sonic's more frequent conformity to the classroom rules. She has capitalised on gendered and racialised stereotypes to form special relationships with practitioners to take advantage of opportunities for positive, individual attention rather than depending on group teaching sessions for her learning.

Sonic has less opportunity for individual support as he seeks fewer interactions with practitioners during the day, depending instead on his relationships with peers as a catalyst for his learning. This is evident both in his outdoor role play and in the classroom activity with construction equipment. When he approaches Mrs. Pandita to discuss his model truck, she is unable to fully support his understanding of addition and position as she is involved with other children. She briefly introduces these concepts by referring to the number of wheels on each side of the vehicle but is distracted before Sonic can fully understand. Compensation for fewer individual interactions with practitioners may be a reason for his greater participation in the group sessions, where he gets affirmation of his learning through acknowledgement of correct answers. Without sustained practitioner interactions it is more difficult for young children to transfer the abstract teaching of addition through written sums on the whiteboard to an understanding of the application of the concept to a concrete situation. Children are then less likely to extend their thinking and understanding beyond what Vygotsky (1986) refers to as the zone of proximal development. This is apparent during Sonic's brief interactions with the teacher: he is left confused as Mrs. Pandita's attention is drawn to the maths activity at the whiteboard. This prevents meaningful discussion regarding the positioning of the wheels.

Kylie is able to explore concepts through situated experiential learning in the outdoor kite play. She stays close to the adult as they discuss the scientific concepts of force during attempts to fly the kite. Sonic does not benefit from such adult interaction when he socialises with a group of boys developing their fantasy play. The *EPPE* Report (2004) introduced the term sustained shared thinking to describe the desired level and quality of interactions between practitioners and children as they engage in play activities. Sustained shared thinking can be achieved through interactions that promote problem solving as well as evaluating and extending play narratives in relation to planned learning objectives (Kingdon, 2014). During periods timetabled for play, the practitioners support the learning of small groups in reading and maths activities. At this time the emphasis on the more managerial curriculum prevent opportunities for Kylie and Sonic to extend learning through their chosen activities with the snails and vehicle construction respectively. Although there are times allocated during the day for children to follow their own interests, opportunities to enhance their learning are missed as priority is given to meet the demands of a managerial pedagogy.

Pedagogical relevance for application of socio-cultural experiences to learning

Extended periods of open-ended play offer opportunities for high-quality interactions to support learning as well as for children to contribute their cultural experiences and interests as they collaborate with the community of learners in the early years classroom (Broadhead and Burt, 2012). Play enables children to explore the environment and develop in context with their personal socio-cultural experiences, as discussed in Devon's story (Chapter 3). This is an alternative to environments based on institutionally accepted cultural norms and hierarchical determination of valuable knowledge. Playful pedagogy contrasts with more formal pedagogical approaches and supports children to understand experiences from home and their own worlds in relation to the new environment of the school. The revised EYFS curriculum places importance on play for young children's learning and development. However, the value of self-directed activity is minimised as children reach the reception class in favour of a focus on achievement and assessment in the prioritised subjects of literacy and mathematics:

> Each area of learning and development must be implemented through planned, purposeful play and through a mix of adult-led and child-initiated activity. Play is essential for children's development, building their confidence as they learn to explore, to think about problems, and relate to others. Children learn by leading their own play, and by taking part in play, which is guided by adults. There is an ongoing judgement to be made by practitioners about the balance between activities led by children, and activities led or guided by adults. . . . As children grow older, and as their development allows, it is expected that the balance will gradually shift towards more activities led by adults, to help children prepare for more formal learning, ready for Year 1.
>
> *(DfE, 2017b, p. 9)*

Although the above paragraph recognises the value of play to children's learning, the sentiment creates a conflict for practitioners through the idea that this should be balanced with 'guided' activity to meet set objectives for assessment. It is recommended that assessment of children's learning should take as little time as possible away from 'high quality interaction' with the children during play (DfE, 2017a, p. 19). However, judgements across the range of subject areas and the assessment methods required for evidence inevitably make this difficult (2017a). The resulting managerial culture leaves practitioners little time to consider the particular needs of children, including those from othered communities. This illustrates how institutional factors, such as accountability, limit inclusion for young black children, impacting on their educational development.

The relevance of play to black children's learning and development is indicated in Sonic's activity with his peers. In the playground they share the British dimensions of their diverse cultures when they collaborate by adapting Mario Brothers electronic games and the superhero television programmes they access at home. The group is able to select common cultural experiences alongside the unique representations of their heritage cultures, such as dialects of English spoken in the home. These opportunities enable them to assert newly forming identities as black British children. Cognitively, they are able to apply emergent literacy skills, to read the map on the outside wall in context with their role play, rather than abstractly in the group literacy sessions that are isolated from their everyday experiences. Group play offers Sonic a more holistic learning experience as the role play develops, rather than the segmented learning through teacher direction in the classroom that is detached from his socio-cultural context and so less meaningful. The shared and unique cultural experiences of Sonic and his peers are catalysts for their elaborate fantasy and are essential as they allow children to develop their own knowledge within their familiar social contexts (McDowall Clark, 2017). Conceptual understanding is then embedded through opportunities to explore learning independently while applying cultural knowledge to new situations. In contrast, Kylie relies on an adult to determine much of her activity during outdoor play. She enjoys the kite flying initiated by Mrs. Paterson to explore planned scientific and environmental concepts of wind and forces. The active experience enables concrete conceptual understanding rather than introduction through abstract representations in whole class teaching sessions. However, the outcome-led play activity does not permit Kylie access to opportunities for independent learning and cultural expression in the same way as for Sonic when developing imaginative play through collaboration with peers. She breaks away from the activity to observe a group of boys playing football. Although she doesn't join in, she indicates her familiarity with football by refereeing the game, representing her knowledge from home in this imaginary situation. She is also able to control the group for a period of ten minutes, asserting a dominant female role, counteracting the stereotypical image of dependency and neediness she portrays when with practitioners.

Other children in this book also benefit from self-directed activity. Pina's narrative (Chapter 5) tells of her making patties during café role play. She speaks in dialect during extended periods available for play, when learning is not always supervised or controlled by practitioners. Her play with Dawn, her teacher, regarding the patties and biscuits that she makes give opportunities for sustained learning of mathematical concepts in context with the role play. Both adult interaction and children's socio-cultural contexts are important to their play as they impact positively on children's dispositions to both their learning and themselves as learners (McDowall Clark, 2017). In another school, Louis represents time spent in his father's garage through play with toy vehicles enhanced by books about cars in the reading area. Victor, his teacher, balances demands for accountability with short structured teaching sessions while allowing the majority of time for child-initiated activity. Jason, in St. Zita, is able to voice a possible conflict with his religious experiences, which are Christian in school and at home Muslim, by making a cross '*for Jesus*' with wooden construction blocks. When alone in narrative role play, he uses the cross as a prop while at the same time representing a visit to the mosque. These opportunities can support black children to express discontinuities between home and school. They can then begin to understand and manage any conflict of cultures to conform to institutional cultural norms. Without these opportunities children may relegate their cultural identities established in the home through double-consciousness. The habituation to two different cultural worlds can cause stress as they conform to hierarchical expectations of whiteness to be good learners.

Parental views on early years pedagogy

In Sonic and Kylie's school, the more formal objective-led early years pedagogy could have emerged in response to English government policy of accountability and outcomes alongside a response to what many black parents in the school value as appropriate teaching methods. The school places importance on involving parents in the education of their children and listens to their views. Parents play strategic as well as practical roles by participating in social and procedural decision-making committees. Parents from black and minority ethnic (BME) communities can prefer more structured approaches to learning with the relevance of play not seen as significant to the achievement of their children (Brooker, 2010; Wood, 2010). One reason for this may be a lack of confidence in the English education system through reports on the underachievement of black pupils. Access to information is widely accessible through the publication of league tables and exclusion rates, along with media narratives of black pupils' disaffection with school (Chapter 7). In this study, parents voiced appreciation of some aspects of the informality of the early years phase in education, with the adjunct that they would have liked more concrete evidence of achievement in maths and literacy. Structured homework was suggested as a practical way of supporting their children's progress. Both Sonic's and Kylie's parents purchased home learning schemes to support their children in the evenings and weekends as homework was not given by the school. Some black parents turn to supplementary schools and private tuition to enhance children's education in the basic subjects (Reay and Mirza, 2001). As soon as Sonic is 5 years old, his parents plan for him to join his older brother for one evening a week at private maths lessons held in a church hall.

Parents also share counter-narratives of family and community experiences, placing responsibility on schools for the particular experiences of black children at institutional and personal levels. By recognising race and racism as a reality, CRT contests the meritocratic concept that black pupils have equal opportunities through the same educational choices as other children. Alternative voices heard through counter-stories allow for an understanding of how discrimination in education is reproduced through the status quo (Gillborn, 2016). Analysis through this perspective can facilitate counterarguments that defend the positions of othered communities. Many black parents believe individual teachers, institutionalised racism in schools and low expectations discriminate against their children (Majors et al., 2001; Rollock et al., 2015). Parents find ways to challenge disadvantage in mainstream education, one of which is through supplementary schools. These alternative institutions aim to ensure that the curriculum content includes their children's cultural knowledge and heritage, considered as critical to their education (Graham, 2001).

EYFS assessment guidance emphasises the importance of involving parents from 'ethnic minorities' in the education of their children in the early years:

> A practitioner's relationship with parents is crucial to developing knowledge of the child and the practitioner's ability to make an accurate assessment. Parents can help practitioners understand the values that explain their child's responses to the environment and social situations.
>
> *(DfE, 2017a, p. 20)*

The document points out the value of links with home to understand each child in context within the social worlds of their cultural heritage, supporting practitioners to value and build on experiences they bring to the setting. The hidden curriculum that marginalises children can then be challenged to provide learning environments that are inclusive of their home cultures and beliefs as essential starting points from which to build understanding. However, it may not be enough to provide for the cultural backgrounds of the children through curriculum activities without critical reflection on how institutional and personal interactions can influence inequalities.

Multiculturalism and whiteness: the experiences of othering

The possibility of multicultural education becoming tokenistic is explored further in Chapter 7 but it is discussed here as an important influence on Kylie's and Sonic's early education experiences. Multiculturalism can lead to a colour-blind impression of unity where difference does not matter, thus ignoring tensions between and within differences (Ladson-Billings and Tate IV, 2006). A more critical multiculturalism is evident in Frankfield School during the whole school assembly attended by Kylie and Sonic. Although the assembly does not directly address racism, acknowledgement of the significance of identity for social and educational opportunities is evident through references to all children's rights for educational equality and success. The head teacher's comments reflect the view that black children may have to work harder to gain academic success due to discriminatory factors both in and outside the school. Parents are invited to the assembly in recognition of a commitment towards ensuring the community has a voice in the school that is inclusive of all cultural and religious perspectives. The importance of education and expectations that all children can achieve their goals by overcoming barriers is reflected in the entrance hall display. Posters of renowned world leaders promoting human rights are displayed to create an ethos of positivity, inspiring challenges to social and economic obstacles towards equality. The displays also indicate an awareness of how racism can create social disadvantage for many of the children in the school and a commitment to academic success that the head teacher believes can give them '*chances in life*'. For Kylie and Sonic, recognition of blackness being valued and articulating the need to challenge racial inequalities can be positive influences on their learning dispositions at the start of education.

Consideration of home experiences and parental involvement encourages links between school, home and community, diffusing the emotional repercussions of possible double-consciousness (Leonardo, 2009). The ethos is supplemented through the demographics of the whole school staff team that reflects the diverse cultural backgrounds of the children, providing good role models of success and positive influences. Personal experiences of the team enable understanding processes of racialisation in education that can be applied in practice to establish a more inclusive environment.

To be successful at including all pupils, schools require more than tokenistic policies and slogans towards equality. Inclusive practices must be included in each classroom as well as through the general school ethos if they are to be effective. Multiculturalism can support a more inclusive education when approached through a pedagogy guided by principles that build on children's socio-cultural experiences as a starting point for mainstream curriculum delivery. Celebrations of cultural festivals are well-meaning activities that can become tokenistic outside an anti-racist frame that encourages children to discuss attitudes towards religions and cultures. This is particularly significant during the current rise in racist attacks reported widely in the media. It is important to talk about these incidents to support children who experience racism and also to those who are exposed to racist attitudes in their homes and communities. They need support to understand the impact of racism on themselves and others. Young children cannot respect other cultures as required in the EYFS curriculum without a critical understanding of how learned negative stereotypes impact on their own lives and society generally.

Kylie and Sonic sit through the assembly concentrating on the depiction of Diwali by Year 5, which is supported in the classroom curriculum through making Diwali lamps (divas) as an important element of the festival. This is planned in isolation to mainstream activities aimed at meeting curriculum outcomes measured in assessment profiles. In this way the positive ethos of the school is somewhat countered in Kylie and Sonic's reception classroom as the environment reflects whiteness in the general resourcing of activities and the visual images displayed. An emphasis on cultural diversity in multiculturalism can become a superficial attempt at challenging inequalities if it does not address the ethos of whiteness maintained in the classroom through everyday practices. Black children starting school can be faced with an environment predetermined by new cultural meanings that are reinforced by images and practices representative of that singular culture. A failure to represent their existence is just one example of environmental racial micro-aggressions that many black children experience in schools. Whiteness is consequentially normalised by an invisibility of blackness in the classroom, through classroom procedures, curriculum and social norms (Robinson and Jones Diaz, 2006). An example of this process of normalisation is when, in Pina's story (Chapter 5), she has no alternative images in the available catalogues for making collages. The only pictures available are those of white girls with long, straight blonde hair. Not only does this reinforce the image of [white people's] straight hair as beautiful, but also the omission of black children can add to the invisibility of her identity. When Petra, the nursery nurse, discusses the collages with Pina and Mariam, her comments do not indicate an awareness of the predominance of whiteness in the images to counteract marginalisation of the identities of the two girls. Absence or denial of identifiable images in resources can create an invisibility that isolates social and cultural experiences from home as well as confirming a position as the other in the racial hierarchy of the school community (Bridgeman, 2011). Resources available to Pina and some other children in this study reflect a colour-blind pedagogy that reproduces the hidden curriculum and can unintentionally exclude children who do not identify with the norms of whiteness in the school.

Summary

Kylie and Sonic demonstrate how they use their agency to access learning experiences by understanding their relationships with practitioners and recognising opportunities to participate in activities that are appropriate for their different dispositions. For Kylie this means ensuring individual attention from an adult for sustained interactions by capitalising on a racialised and gendered notion of her identity. This makes her appear to be emotionally needy and requiring additional support to give her confidence. Her story contradicts this through her subtle breaking of classroom rules and her ability to control a large group of boys in their game of football. Sonic finds it easier to gain attention by participating in class group sessions while conforming to expectations of behaviour to access learning opportunities. He actively contradicts the stereotype of disruptive behaviour assigned to many black boys. He has little contact with adults during independent play periods, approaching a practitioner only when he needs to clarify a mathematical concept of which he is unsure. He takes the opportunity to use imaginative play to affirm his identity through interactions with peers, indicating the importance of play to enable black children to represent their cultural understandings.

Both children have strong black identities that are supported by the ethos in the school and the many black children in the classroom. However, norms of whiteness in the early years curriculum can be unintentionally reproduced through interpretations of multiculturalism that emphasise rather than include difference. Educational aims that are measured only by developmental norms can act to marginalise children's individual needs. Classrooms offering children opportunities for independent, self-initiated activity through playful pedagogy can allow for them to find new meanings to their black identities. Their socio-cultural experiences can then support interactions with others as they explore new ideas and concepts. This gives value and meaning to their home cultures in an environment where they may otherwise feel disconnected through the dominance of whiteness in institutional practices.

Reflective practice

• What might be the implications of children's differing learning styles for practitioners in relation to classroom organisation and curriculum delivery?

• Consider how black children can be racialised in your setting through curriculum content and resourcing.

• How can your setting create an ethos that challenges whiteness and affirms black children's identities?

References

Bradbury, A. (2013) *Understanding Early Years Inequality: Policy, Assessment and Young Children's Identities.* Oxon: Routledge.

Bridgeman, J. (2011) African American Counter Narratives, in Zamudio, M., Russell, C., Rios, F. and Bridgeman, J. (eds.), *Critical Race Theory Matters: Education and Ideology.* Oxon: Routledge.

Broadhead, P. and Burt, A. (2012) *Understanding Young Children's Learning through Play.* Oxon: Routledge.

Brooker, L. (2010) Learning to Play in a Cultural Context, in Broadhead, P., Howard, J. and Wood, E. (eds.), *Play and Learning in the Early Years.* London: Sage Publications.

DfE (2017a) *Early Years Foundation Stage Profile Handbook.* London: Her Majesty's Stationary Office.

DfE (2017b) *Statutory Framework for the Early Years Foundation Stage: Setting the Standards for Learning, Development and Care for Children from Birth to Five.* London: Her Majesty's Stationary Office.

Gillborn, D. (2016) *White Lies: Things That Were Told about Race and Education That Weren't True.* Available from www.birmingham.ac.uk/schools/education/research/2016/gillborn. Accessed 19 October 2016.

Graham, M. (2001) The Mis-Education of Black Children in the British Education System, in Majors, R. (ed.), *Educating Our Black Children: New Directions and Radical Approaches.* Oxon: Routledge.

Kingdon, Z. (2014) Research-Informed Policy – Myth or Reality? Sustained Shared Thinking, in Kingdon, Z. and Gourd, J. (eds.), *Early Years Policy: The Impact on Practice.* Oxon: Routledge.

Ladson-Billings, G. and Tate IV, W. F. (2006) Toward a Critical Race Theory of Education, in Dixson, A. and Rousseau, C. (eds.), *Critical Race Theory in Education.* Oxon: Routledge.

Lea, S. (2014) Early Years Work, Professionalism and the Translation of Policy into Practice, in Kingdon, Z. and Gourd, J. (eds.), *Early Years Policy: The Impact on Practice.* Oxon: Routledge.

Leonardo, Z. (2009) The Color of Supremacy, in Taylor, E., Gillborn, D. and Ladson-Billings, G. (eds.), *Foundations of Critical Race Theory in Education.* Oxon: Routledge.

Majors, R., Wilkinson, V. and Gulan, W. (2001) Mentoring Black Males: Responding to the Crisis in Education and Social Alienation, in Majors, R. (ed.), *Educating Our Black Children: New Directions and Radical Approaches.* Oxon: Routledge.

McDowall Clark, R. (2017) *Exploring the Contexts for Early Learning: Challenging the School Readiness Agenda.* Oxon: Routledge.

Qualifications, Curriculum and Assessment Authority (QCA) (2003) *Foundation Stage Profile.* London: QCA Publications.

Reay, D. and Mirza, H. (2001) Black Supplementary Schools, in Majors, R. (ed.), *Educating Our Black Children*. London: Routledge Falmer.

Robinson, K. and Jones Diaz, C. (2006) *Diversity and Difference in Early Childhood Education*. Berkshire: Open University Press.

Rollock, N., et al. (2015) *The Colour of Class*. Oxon: Routledge.

Rowan, L. and Honan, E. (2005) Literarily Lost: The Quest for Quality Literacy Agendas in Early Childhood Education, in Yelland, N. (ed.), *Critical Issues in Early Childhood Education*. Berkshire: Open University Press.

Sewell, T. (1996) *Black Masculinities and Schooling: How Black Boys Survive Modern Schooling*. Staffordshire: Trentham Books.

Siraj-Blatchford, I. and Siraj-Blatchford, J. (2007) An Ethnographic Approach to Researching Young Children's Learning, in MacNaughton, G., Rolfe, S. and Siraj-Blatchford, I. (eds.), *Doing Early Childhood Research*. Berkshire: Open University Press.

Sylva, K., et al. (2004) *The Effective Provision of Pre-School Education (EPPE): Final Report*. London: Institute of Education.

Vygotsky, L. (1986) *Thought and Language*. Cambridge, MA, USA: The MIT Press.

Wood, E. (2010) Reconceptualizing the Play-Pedagogy Relationship, in Brooker, L. and Edwards, S. (eds.), *Engaging Play*. Berkshire: Open University Press.

Wright, C., Weekes, D. and McGlaughlin, A. (2000) *Race, Class and Gender in Exclusions from School*. London: Falmer Press.

Wright, C., Weekes, D. and McGlaughlin, A. (2006) Gender Blind Racism and the Experience of Schooling and Identity Formation, in Arnot, M. and Mac an Ghail, M. (eds.), *Gender and Education*. Oxon: Routledge.

5

PINA'S STORY – A 'GOOD HAIR' DAY?

Racialisation of the black child through physical appearance

Introduction

Pina's story tells of her experiences during the second half term in school and how her hair is a primary signifier of her racialised identity. Her story is not untypical of others in the study whose hair, as for many young black children, has contributed to their racialisation. The narrative indicates how they are othered in the classroom by negative stereotypes connected to physical appearance focused on hair texture and styling. Individual racial micro-aggressions are often disbelieved or deemed insignificant by those outside marginalised communities. The timescale of the events in Pina's story has been shortened to make apparent the impact of daily racial micro-aggressions experienced by black children through comments and actions of others towards hair. From a position of whiteness, micro-aggressions can be perceived as imagined racism or directed at the recipient without racist intent. The time-compression technique used in fictional composite narratives can better convey the impact of daily micro-aggressions, both intentional and non-intentional, that contribute to the racialisation of young black children. Composite narratives representing racialising experiences challenge the taken for granted understandings of those at the centre of both personal and institutional whiteness to inform inclusive learning environments that support black children as they begin their education (Solorzano and Yosso, 2009).

Researcher interpretations of racialisation through physical appearance in Pina's story are inevitably influenced by a perspective of a personal history of whiteness. This can be challenged through a CRT lens by centralising racism as an overarching factor impacting on social relationships. Accepting the significance of racism in data analysis can enable interpretation from a positioning of whiteness to be questioned. To further counteract bias, voices from the black community regarding their personal experiences have been included to reflect on how the morning events contribute to Pina's racialisation. Through a CRT tenet of listening to the counter-narratives of those who experience racism, it is possible to dismiss pejorative views of the insignificance of racial micro-aggressions, which can be voiced through whiteness as 'imagined', 'harmless' and 'innocent' (Sue, 2010). Young children are capable of manipulating situations to their advantage in response to raced and gendered adult expectations, as children as young as 3 have been observed to 'employ racial and ethnic concepts as important integrative and symbolically creative tools in the daily construction of their social lives' (Van Ausdale and Feagin, 2001, p. 26). Pina's story tells how her interactions with peers contribute to the racial micro-aggressions she experiences in the new social world of the classroom. Essed (2013) explains micro-aggressions as the daily drip-drip effects of racism experienced through everyday interactions.

Pina's story

It is a spring morning in a three-bedroom flat on Stockbridge Estate in a multiracial borough of a large English city. Four-year-old Pina is a black British girl with Jamaican heritage. She is eating her breakfast with her two older brothers while her mother, Josephina, is frantically looking for her book bag and getting her own things together for college. Josephina has been caring for Pina since her mother, Josephina's sister, became homeless 2 years ago as a result of mental illness. She has officially adopted Pina and, now that she has started school, Josephina is able to restart the childcare course she began a few years ago. The children finish eating and rush around the flat collecting their things for school.

Josephina is angry because last night she found Pina cutting chunks of her own hair when she should have been in bed sleeping. Pina gave no explanation and Josephina is upset that she wanted to cut her hair when friends and family admired it for being so thick, curly and long. Josephina styles Pina's hair for school in the usual two large bunches and asks her again why she had cut it. Pina still refuses to answer and sits quietly, near to tears, as her mother angrily pulls the bunches into bands. Josephina threatens to tell the reception class teacher, Dawn, what Pina had done if she will not talk about it with her. They all gather in the hall to leave the house. Pina looks sad and drags behind the family group as they hurry along the busy road to reach school before the bell goes at nine o'clock. They hear the bell ringing as they turn the corner and approach the building. Pina is still walking behind the others as they enter the large playground. Brandon waves goodbye as he approaches the separate Junior school entrance, while Dean shouts 'bye' as he runs to his classroom. Josephina and Pina walk round to the reception class entrance. The four reception classes are situated on the ground floor having direct access to the playground. Josephina takes Pina's hand and leads her into her classroom, approaching Dawn, the teacher, to inform her of Pina's moodiness being a result of the hair-cutting episode. She then kisses Pina goodbye and leaves for college.

Pina stands alone quietly, feeling sad about the quarrel with her mother. She looks expectantly at Dawn, who is too busy with other parents and children to pay her immediate attention. After a few minutes Pina relaxes as she realises that Dawn is not going to discuss the hair-cutting incident. She looks around the classroom for her best friend, Mariam, and joins her in the café role-play area where they make cookies together, laughing and chatting as they bake. The majority of the thirty children in the class have Asian cultural backgrounds, while Pina is one of two black girls with African-Caribbean heritage. She has a special relationship with Mariam, whose parents are originally from Sri-Lanka. They are playing in the café when Dawn calls them to join the whole class on the carpet. They sit together listening intently as Dawn informs the class of the day's activities. Pina feels someone gently pulling her bunches. She turns round and looks crossly at Savita and Rucksana, who are acting innocent. She turns back and feels her hair pulled again. She shouts out angrily for them to stop and they giggle quietly. Dawn asks Pina what is wrong and she tells her that the two girls are pulling her hair and will '*not stop*'! Dawn impatiently instructs Pina to concentrate on the phonics lesson, without confronting her distress or linking her annoyance with the incident at home. Pina turns to Savita and Rucksana and gives them a threatening look, which they ignore, smiling together. However, they do not touch her hair again and Pina joins in the lesson, being praised for giving the correct answer on one occasion. She hugs Mariam in pleasure at the praise.

It is playtime in the large Infant playground and there is pop and rap music playing on the wooden stage. Pina rushes straight over, with Mariam following, and they begin to dance. Pina sees Remmie coming out of her classroom and calls her over to dance to the music. Remmie is a black girl with the same Jamaican heritage as Pina. She is new to the school and although they are in different reception classes, they always play together in break times. As they laugh and dance, Pina calls out to a practitioner who is close by that this music is played in her house and that her favourite is Michael Jackson's song 'Thriller'. She breakdances to the next tune, laughing with Remmie. Mariam sits on the stage watching them as they dance until the bell goes at the end of playtime. The three girls go back inside, talking excitedly together as they hang up their coats, and say goodbye to Remmie who goes to her adjacent classroom.

In the classroom Pina sits next to Mariam as the children gather together in a circle on the carpet to eat their daily piece of fruit. She tells Petra, a practitioner, that she likes her hair, which is blond, straight and shoulder length. She asks Petra to twist her hair in bunches, which she does as Pina eats her tangerine. When Petra finishes the twists, Pina flicks them from side to side. She finishes eating her tangerine and goes alone to the café to make patties with the play dough. She rolls the dough flat, uses a circular plate to cut around and carefully folds the dough circles in half, fitting two on each plate to put in the oven to cook. She talks in Jamaican dialect to an imaginary companion about what she is doing, including how she is making the patties '*pepper*' [spicy/hot] '*but not for baby*'.

Mariam joins her after five minutes to ask her to make pictures in the creative area. They sit at a table surrounded by felt tips, glue sticks, scissors and magazines and skilfully begin to cut out pictures of white girls with long blond hair chosen from the pages of toy catalogues. They talk admiringly about the girls' hair and costumes as they carefully select, cut out and arrange the images, glueing them onto their individual collages. When finished, they take the pictures over to Petra, who comments on the *'beautiful'* princesses and fairy dresses in the images and asks Pina to sound out the word 'dress' phonetically. Pina ignores the request and walks away to make more patties in the café. Petra continues to read with Mariam in the literacy area, while Pina invites Dawn into the café for dinner. Dawn takes the role of customer and Pina writes her order on a piece of paper, then serves her with the patties she previously made until it is time to sit in a class group again for a numeracy lesson.

Pina and Mariam go to the carpet, choosing to sit away from Savita and Rucksana at the back close to Petra. They sit concentrating on the rhyme and props used to convey an understanding of number to ten. Petra moves to the other side of the group to support a child who is not concentrating. Rizwan, who is sitting behind Pina, gently touches her hair and then touches Mariam's, silently comparing the textures. Pina turns to tell him to stop pulling her hair. She complains to Dawn, who instructs her to concentrate on the lesson and then asks her a question about the group activity, which Pina cannot answer. Pina sits quietly listening without participating until it is lunchtime and the children are asked to wash their hands.

Having eaten lunch, Pina, Mariam and Remmie are outside playing with a large group of girls from the reception year group. They form long lines joined by holding their wool scarves, while they run together across the large playground, laughing and shouting in enjoyment. The group breaks up and the three friends go to the climbing apparatus where there is a group of older boys from Years 1 and 2. As the girls begin to climb the frame, three of the boys shout at them to go away because *'it's for boys'*. Remmie gets off the frame but Pina and Mariam continue to climb, laughing together and ignoring the shouts. A white boy laughs and insults Pina's hair, which is now back in two bunches as the twists have come undone. She gets off the climbing frame and the other two girls follow as she runs over to the only black practitioner, Charmaine. Pina is tearful as she points to the boys on the climbing frame and repeats the boy's insult: *'that's the stupidest hair ever'*. Charmaine comforts her, telling her that she has lovely hair and not to take any notice. Pina runs back to the climbing frame with Mariam and Remmie and shouts out to the boys, who ignore her. They do not attempt to climb again but run off to play with a group of girls in another part of the playground until it is time to go into the class for the afternoon session.

Reflections on Pina's story

The social context of black children's experiences of racialisation

The narrative begins with Pina's family engaged in the morning rush typical of many homes when children are getting ready for school and parents are preparing for their own busy days. Josephina is a single mother who, despite being well organised, still has to deal with the last-minute preparations of her three children for school. Pina is adopted by Josephina and has been living with the family for 2 years. Josephina is pleased that she has started her college course again, as she has been frustrated with being at home for the last 2 years until Pina started school. However, for a woman on her own with family responsibilities and a limited budget, any new problems can cause additional stress. The social context of children's lives is not limited to social relationships but is interconnected with political and economic factors that discriminate against particular groups in society. This perpetuates hierarchies of advantage and disadvantage based on the intersections of race with class and gender. Establishing different forms of communication with parents and carers in schools can facilitate an understanding of social factors that impinge on black children's lives and subsequently on their education. Opportunities should be offered in all early years settings to speak to parents daily to hear the daily realities and concerns of family life as they inevitably affect the children in school.

The importance of daily communication has been understood by the management team at Pina's school through a more flexible, fifteen-minute timescale during which children come to school before morning registration. This staggered entry period goes some way to alleviating the stress of the morning responsibilities for families. The more flexible routine also facilitates communication between practitioners and parents, allowing for a better understanding of the child in relation to both home and school. During this time, Josephina was briefly able to tell Dawn about the incident of hair-cutting being the reason for Pina's mood. Without sufficient time or opportunities for discussion with parents, practitioners can remain unaware of the circumstances that impinge on children's development. Viewed out of context, lateness can be attributed to stereotypes around 'black indolence and tardiness', which are historically based attitudes perpetuated through stereotypes of black women as unfit mothers and as being inadequate in relation to white societal values such as punctuality (Ladson-Billings, 2009, p. 89). Negative stereotypes of black families prevail across social classes. Rollock et al. (2015) found that middle-class professional parents experience stereotypes of being uninterested in their children's education and as being inadequate families. Opinions can be formed from racialised notions of all black families as deficient rather than knowledge and understanding of the socio-economic conditions that challenge some black families (Bradbury, 2013). Other children in the project, Shania and Jason, were often late. Practitioners were unaware that Shania's father had left home and that her uncle had moved in, causing additional stress on the family that inevitably impacted on the morning routine. Jason was also frequently late as his mother, who had recently been hospitalised, was often alone in the mornings to get two children ready for school as well as having a toddler with chickenpox at that time. The staggered timescale for arriving at school affords opportunities for discussion between parents and practitioners. By forming trusting relationships through meaningful interactions, practitioners can gain an understanding of family life, challenging harmful stereotypes. Communication regarding issues affecting circumstances can then reduce parental concerns, such as stigmatisation as latecomers, avoiding additional stress on families.

Pina's narrative demonstrates how the flexible morning classroom routine enables Josephina to alert the practitioners to Pina's moodiness as a result of the hair-cutting episode. Despite this, Dawn does not take the opportunity to discuss this further with Pina and her mother. This may be because she is managing the busy demands of the classroom, such as class size and the need to respond to many parents during this period. Current responsibilities arising from the managerial culture in education make heavy claims on practitioner time. Administrative requirements for accountability through assessments, curriculum planning documentation, and record-keeping take attention away from what is seen by practitioners as really mattering in early years education. Opportunities are reduced not only for communication with parents but also for interaction with children during their exploration and learning activity throughout the day. Curriculum initiatives and requirements restrict time to observe and discuss children's individual progress and how learning can be extended through children's own interests rather than through an over-formalised curriculum (McDowall Clark, 2017). In addition to managerial responsibilities and curriculum initiatives being reasons for the lack of support for Pina, Dawn is not able to understand the implications of spoken and unspoken micro-aggressions (Chapter 3. Her position of whiteness prevents Dawn seeing the incident as racism, as discussed further in her own story (Chapter 6).

Experiences of racialisation through hierarchies of beauty

Young black children can enter school with positive social experiences and emotions regarding themselves, as they may not have been widely exposed to or internalised negative attitudes in society. Hair plays an important part of the relationship between the black child and the family, with much positive social time spent grooming and styling. Clarke's narrative (1983, p. 3) indicates the importance of this to acquisition of her cultural identity and wealth when growing up. She explains how these occasions 'taught me art, gave me good advice, gave me language, made me love something about myself'. It can emotionally impact on black children when negativity is directed at them regarding their appearance once they enter the world outside their home. Rock tells of this in the documentary *Good Hair* (Stilson, 2009) when his 3-year-old daughter tearfully asks him why her hair is not 'good hair'. The term is sometimes used in the African-Caribbean/American community to describe hair in context with attributes of whiteness, idealising straighter hair as beautiful in contradiction to the natural curls of black women (Tatum, 1997, p. 45; Clarke, 1983, p. 2; hooks, 1993, p. 86; Tate, 2009). Rock was surprised, as he was previously unaware that his daughter had internalised these racialised attitudes regarding hair as she had only received positive and affirmative comments in the home. However, social norms and power relations of whiteness in a racialised society can negate these positive messages, as Rollock demonstrates in a personal narrative of her school experiences:

> Hair was a subject of white curiosity. How often did I wash it? How long did it take to style and in moments that struck an, as yet un-analysed peril in my heart, could they touch it? While white girls flicked their hair or dried it in seconds under the dryer when we went swimming, I and the other Black girls attempted to restore ours to some natural order before, the job yet incomplete, being barked back into hurried lines by impatient gym teachers. . . . These daily moments of othering were not limited to the relatively unmonitored spaces of the playground but were also evident within the classroom.
>
> *(Rollock, 2012, p. 77)*

The colour-blindness of Rollock's teachers prevented them from giving time and space for the black girls to adjust their hair, as the organisation of time was perceived from a position of whiteness. Pina experiences acts of racialised othering throughout the day by incidents of her hair being touched by other children when sitting in the whole class teaching sessions. Other children in the study, Louis, Shania and Devon, also voiced distress when their hair was pulled or touched by their peers when sitting in a group of children. Reactions such as Pina cutting her hair could be emotional responses to the touching of hair and the effect of numerous seemingly insignificant micro-aggressions and othering experiences. Essed (2013) sees these as contributing to everyday racism where the dominance of whiteness in society leaves nowhere to hide. This form of interactional, inescapable racism can be a source of stress and impact on self-esteem and identity.

Incidents of touch can be viewed as normal behaviours in young children through their curiosity to explore textures, as encouraged in the EYFS science curriculum (Nutbrown, 1996). This could be the reason for Rizwan gently feeling the hair of Pina and Mariam in turn. However, the reactions of Pina and the other children appear to have a different, more emotional significance for black children, as they may experience this as a micro-assault on their person. Counter-narratives told in Stilson's documentary (2009) give voice to how the touching of black women's hair is unacceptable, with narrators being adamant that their hair is not to be approached by anyone unless given permission. While recognising incidents of spontaneous touch may be because of 'white people's curiosity', it can also be attributed to entrenched attitudes which psychologically still view black people as property; consequently there exists a right to touch without consent (Ladson-Billlings, 2009, p. 25). Actions towards black people are thus determined through hierarchies of whiteness historically originating from ownership in times of slavery. This inherent manifestation of racism is disempowering, as it negates black people's rights to make decisions.

A more overt form of micro-assault experienced by Pina occurs in the playground when a white boy uses strategic racist name-calling (Troyna and Hatcher,

1992) to deliberately upset her by saying that she has the 'stupidest hair ever'. Perhaps from a perspective of accepted norms of beauty, the white boy has already understood the interracial connotations of such a phrase, using it intentionally as a strategy to make her withdraw from the apparatus. Black children as young as 3 can understand racialisation through physical appearance as being normal, having internalised negative remarks regarding their natural hair through dominant discourses of whiteness as beauty (Tate, 2009). Recurring attitudes such as those in the playground are likely to impact on Pina's identity as she is exposed in school to the reality of her hair not being valued within the domination of whiteness as the desirable norm, possibly forcing a wider evaluation of her own body. These ideas are not likely to stop at hair but can include other physical characteristics of the black child such as skin tone and facial features, as experienced by black practitioners in the study. The incident in the playground could add to and consolidate previous experiences of racialisation and exclusion, possible reasons for Pina cutting her own hair. Her action could be alternatively interpreted as a consequence of early socialisation into a hierarchy of whiteness where the texture of her hair is not valued. Perhaps Pina's comments to Petra that she likes her long blond hair are a consequence of the desirability placed on such hair that is also reinforced through depictions in the catalogues that Pina uses for her collage. Tate (2009) and hooks (1993) consider the numerous micro-invalidations of their appearance through everyday incidents as resulting in self-hate and internalised racism, which they voice as common emotions for black people.

A reason for Josephina's distress may be an understanding that for Pina the act of cutting her hair is the beginning of a recognition of racialisation and othering of her appearance, which Josephina may recall from her own childhood. The process of internalising racism can begin early, as demonstrated in DuBois' account of when he first became aware of racism as a young child during a game played with white peers:

> It is the early days of rollicking boyhood that the revelation first bursts upon one, all in a day, as it were. I remember well when the shadow swept across me. I was a little thing. . . . The exchange was merry, till one girl, a tall newcomer, refused my card – refused it peremptorily, with a glance. Then it dawned upon me with a certain suddenness that I was different from the others.
>
> *(1994, p. 2)*

This is reflective of how black children can feel when first encountering deliberate exclusion. The events may seem innocuous to the white bystander, but for those experiencing them they are profound and often traumatic. During Pina's early experiences of othering, the support from a black practitioner, Charmaine, gives her confidence to challenge the remarks by the boy on the climbing apparatus by returning to shout at the boys. She draws on her resilience to resist the victimisation of the racism she experiences by challenging them.

Seemingly insignificant actions can affect children's relationships with adults as well as peers, as in Clarke's narrative poem of a young black schoolgirl describing racial micro-assaults on her hair:

> Vashti's hair was never straightened
> To be black was bad enough.
> To be black and have nappy hair
> was just plain rough.
> Boys terrorized her,
> Girls scorned her,
> Adults walked the other way
> To avoid the play
> Of Vashti's eyes
> Marking their cruelty.
>
> (1983, p. 8)

The poem indicates how, through adults ignoring the racialised experiences of black children, the emotional pain of racism directed by other children can be reinforced. Hill et al. (2007) found that black pupils had little confidence in their white teachers to address the emotional consequences of racist incidents. Even when approached, the teachers did not support them or challenge the perpetrators. It is sometimes easier to ignore racialised incidents either because of a lack of understanding from a colour-blind perspective or as a decision not to acknowledge they exist in the early years environment. It may sometimes be that when faced with an incident, practitioners are taken by surprise and do not know how to manage the situation because of either their own emotions or those of the children. Dawn was observed some days later complimenting Pina on her neatly plaited hairstyle, which may be well intentioned but which Pina could experience as a micro-aggression. Her more usual unplaited hairstyle is not complimented but her plaits, which are more generally acceptable in society as neat and tidy, receive a compliment (Rollock et al., 2015). This acceptance was echoed in Shania's school when a comment was made that her unplaited hair was always such a mess, insinuating that she is not cared for in the home. Shania had proudly told the researcher earlier in the day that she had done her own hair that morning, in bunches with ribbons, and the lack of neatness could be explained by positive attempts at independence rather than a lack of care. The racialisation of Pina's identity based on her hair as a primary signifier is manifested through her everyday experiences of micro-aggressions, both covert and overt, spoken and unspoken. Racial micro-aggressions can produce a range of both physical and psychological effects on self-esteem and identity. The micro-invalidations and othering of black children in relation to hierarchies of the desirability of physical characteristics of whiteness can also have psychological impact on the relationships with peers and practitioners. Consequences are often reflected through displays of emotion represented by unaccepted modes of behaviour that can lead to a possible later rejection of the norms of school (Tatum, 1997).

Challenging racialised and gendered hierarchies in the classroom

Faced with negative comments from peers regarding her hair, Pina chooses to approach a black practitioner, Charmaine, for reassurance. This may be because Pina already recognises a shared experience of the racialisation of her physical appearance and the personal understanding that Charmaine may bring to her emotional reaction regarding the boy's remark. Another reason for her approach to Charmaine could be due to her experiences of white practitioners not appropriately supporting her emotional distress on previous occasions. Van Ausdale and Feagin's (2001) research indicates preschoolers' awareness of how colour-blindness operates to negate black children's unique racialising experiences; this informs who black children are likely to ask for support when abused. They found that white children as young as 3 insulted black children's hair as well as using other racist terms in the racialised power dynamics of the preschool setting. This is particularly prevalent in outdoor play, where adults cannot always hear, indicating young children's awareness that overt racism is unacceptable in early years settings. As in Pina's situation, verbal racial micro-assaults are used to gain access to equipment as well as to acquire power and exclude children in play situations. This shows an understanding from a young age of the racial rules of behaviour and a sense of the hierarchy of whiteness to control interracial interactions in order to gain white privilege. Pina's hair is targeted for abuse on the climbing frame as a strategy to exclude the two girls from what is commonly perceived as male territory. As well as exposing a gendered hierarchy, this suggests an additional awareness in children of the relevance of hair styling to a female gendered and racialised identity.

Boys in the study also found hair to be a key signifier of a racialised and gendered identity. Louis is observed to be visibly upset on three occasions when he feels violated. He objects strongly to his hair being pulled by a boy in his class. Another boy recognises his distress and reports the incident to a practitioner. On a second occasion, Louis complains to his teacher, Victor, that his hair called a 'pompom', a term connected with female hairstyles. Although both practitioners acknowledge that he was upset, after initial sympathetic remarks the significance of the incidents was not addressed on either occasion through discussion with the children involved or possible curriculum initiatives. One reason for lack of action could be their personal feelings leaving them unprepared or unwilling to understand or discuss the impact of micro-aggressions as they occur. Louis showed extreme distress on a third occasion during a visit to the local library. The practitioner responsible for Louis on the trip had mistaken him for a girl and had been referring to him as 'she' throughout the morning, taking him to the girls' toilets despite his objections. Back in the classroom, Louis complained to Victor in tears and accompanied him as he explained the mistaken identity to the classroom assistant, who responded by laughing and saying that it was because of his hairstyle. No further action was taken to discuss the implications of Louis' mistaken gender identity. This leaves him unsupported even though Victor was aware of the other occasions when Louis was mistaken for a girl. His response to the micro-assaults on Louis' identity is indicative of a denial of the contributions of everyday micro-aggressions to the racialisation of black children. Confusion regarding the intersections of his identity could contribute to Louis' dependence in the classroom on his best friend Lewis, as discussed in Chapter 3. Devon was equally perturbed when his male identity was invalidated by a black peer who laughed at his plaited hairstyle, saying that it looked like *'a girl's hair'*. Devon placed his head on the table and covered his hair with his hands for a few minutes before rejoining the activity. Louis' mother explained to the researcher that it was a cultural practice in some African-Caribbean families not to cut their child's hair until they were fluent speakers, or sometimes older. It is important to be aware of possible cultural rationales in addition to more usual ones of fashion preferences in hair styling when black boys do not have the short hairstyle more traditionally viewed through whiteness as appropriate for school. Black male gendered identity, perceived through the appearance of short hair, conforms to the socially constructed, racialised stereotypes of physically macho images derived historically from slavery (Fletchman-Smith, 2011). Black male identity is rooted in these social constructs that are reinforced through hierarchies of whiteness in school procedures, such as school uniform requirements that include hairstyles. Parents have taken legal action against a school on grounds of racial discrimination, as their son was asked to cut his hair to conform to school uniform standards. The school was refusing to acknowledge long hair as a religious requirement of the Rastafarian religion, seeing it only as a social issue. Such institutional micro-aggressions can create conflict for children who are forming new relationships in school. For Pina, Louis and Devon, hair represents an important element in the formation of their identity, as this aspect of their cultural wealth encompasses emergent racialised and gendered meanings as they socialise at the start of their formal schooling. For them, dominant Eurocentric forms of beauty apparent through hair texture and styling contribute to their everyday negative experiences of racialised and gendered perceptions of the norm.

Early experiences regarding physical characteristics can initiate awareness in both black and white children of power relations in society and a hierarchy of whiteness in the classroom as black children are othered through the racialisation of their appearance. Social positions are understood through early classroom interactions with peers, based on assumed racialised hierarchies reflecting those in society. Taken for granted assumptions in white environments can result in lack of awareness of the black experience in education. Unconscious bias can ensue through acceptance of whiteness as the unspoken and often unrecognised norm, preventing a critical sense of how racism is unintentionally reproduced through classroom interactions. A disconnect from the racialised experiences of others ensues when more pernicious elements of racialisation emerge as part of a young child's experiences but are not recognised or understood. By centralising race through a critical, anti-racist pedagogy, the implications of this form of unintentional racism and accompanying micro-aggressions can be challenged. Listening to the voices of black children can enable interpretation of their experiences in context, with more commonly understood views from positions of whiteness manifested in the hidden curriculum of resources, attitudes and norms of the institution. Alternative perspectives can then be applied to policies and procedures to make changes towards more equitable and socially just learning environments for children. A critical approach can also encourage reflection on personal attitudes such as the effectiveness of a colour-blind approach to multiculturalism that does not address issues of racism directly with young children through the early years curriculum and daily interactions. Additionally, a critical pedagogy challenges preformed racialised attitudes of white children by enabling them to understand reactions and painful emotions arising from incidents of racism. Discussion with children raises awareness of the negative influences their attitudes have on their personal development as well as social relationships in school and wider society. Applied to Pina's experiences, this position could counteract learned, unspoken hierarchal assumptions of physical attributes of whiteness being desirable. At the same time it can reaffirm the positive values acquired by black children of hair and other physical characteristics of blackness.

Summary

Pina's story and the experiences of the other children in the study regarding micro-aggressions directed towards their appearance and identities highlight the importance of understanding how black children may be marginalised in early years classrooms. Her story tells how phenotype remains a key signifier of 'race' despite scientific discreditation of biological theories. Characteristics such as hair and skin colour continue to racialise and other black children within a hierarchy of beauty formed through notions of biological supremacy that are historically based in colonisation, slavery and pseudoscientific theories. Examples of how young children perceive race in social hierarchies negate the colour-blind theory that they are too young to understand the implications and are merely performing mimetic actions. Early years policy and practice can address preformed stereotyped notions of identity through communication with families and colleagues that provides opportunities to understand cultural nuances and the implications of discrimination that pervade all aspects of society. Curriculum resources and content that reflect diversity can raise discussion in an environment organised to give children independence to explore, understand and challenge stereotypes associated with negative attitudes to difference.

Reflective practice

- Consider what possible personal and environmental micro-aggressions in your setting contribute to the racialisation of black children.
- How can children's views on hierarchies of appearance be challenged through opportunities for discussion as part of the curriculum content and organisation?
- Communication with parents, family and community is crucial to young children's well-being. What may be preventing this, and how can procedures and

management of the setting facilitate development of opportunities for meaningful communication?

References

Bradbury, A. (2013) *Understanding Early Years Inequality: Policy, Assessment and Young Children's Identities*. Oxon: Routledge.

Clarke, C. (1983) *Narratives: Poems in the Tradition of Black Women*. New York, USA: Kitchen Table Women of Color Press.

DuBois, W. E. B. (1994) *The Souls of Black Folk*. New York, USA: Dover Publications.

Essed, P. (2013) Keynote Lecture: Everyday Racism and Resistance, in *Proceedings of the Racism and Anti-Racism through Education and Community Practice Conference*, June 26–28, 2013, The Centre for Education for Racial Equality in Scotland: University of Edinburgh, Edinburgh, Scotland.

Fletchman-Smith, B. (2011) *Transcending the Legacies of Slavery*. London: Karnac.

Hill, M., Graham, C., Caulfield, C., Ross, N. and Shelton, A. (2007) Interethnic Relations among Children in School: The Perspectives of Young People in Scotland, in *European Journal of Education*, 42 (2) pp. 267–279.

hooks, B. (1993) *Sisters of the Yam*. Boston, USA: South End Press.

Ladson-Billings, G. (2009) Who You Callin' Nappy-Headed? A Critical Race Theory Look at the Construction of Black Women, in *Race, Ethnicity and Education*, 12 (1) pp. 87–99.

McDowall Clark, R. (2017) *Exploring the Contexts for Early Learning: Challenging the School Readiness Agenda*. Oxon: Routledge.

Nutbrown, C. (1996) Questions for Respectful Educators, in Nutbrown, C. (ed.), *Children's Rights and Early Education*. London: Paul Chapman.

Rollock, N. (2012) The Invisibility of Race: Intersectional Reflections on the Liminal Space of Alterity, in *Race, Ethnicity and Education*, 15 (1) pp. 65–82.

Rollock, N., et al. (2015) *The Colour of Class*. Oxon: Routledge.

Solorzano, G. and Yosso, T. (2009) Critical Race Methodology: Counter-Storytelling as an Analytical Framework for Educational Research, in Taylor, E., Gillborn, D. and Ladson-Billings, G. (eds.), *Foundations of Critical Race Theory in Education*. Oxon: Routledge.

Stilson, J. (2009) *Good Hair*. HBO Films: A Zahrlo and Urban Romances Production, USA.

Sue, D. W. (2010) *Microaggressions in Everyday Life*. Hoboken, New Jersey, USA: Wiley.

Tate, S. A. (2009) *Black Beauty: Aesthetics, Stylization, Politics*. London: Ashgate.

Tatum, B. (1997) *Why Are All the Black Kids Sitting Together in the Cafeteria?* New York, USA: Basic Books.

Troyna, B. and Hatcher, R. (1992) *Racism in Children's Lives: Study of Mainly-White Primary Schools*. London: Routledge/NCB.

Van Ausdale, D. and Feagin, J. R. (2001) *The First R.: How Children Learn Race and Racism*. Lanham, Maryland, USA: Rowman and Littlefield.

6

DAWN'S STORY – 'BUT THAT'S NOT RACIST!'

A white perspective on Pina's story

Introduction

Dawn's story demonstrates the conflict between a commitment to provide equality for all children in a safe learning environment and the reality of discrimination and racialisation through predominant norms of whiteness. Her story gives a practitioner perspective on Pina's experiences of racialisation told in the previous chapter. Dawn attempts to address the concerns of both Pina and her mother from a position of whiteness. The story is told from a premise that majority white stories can contribute to understanding how whiteness and white privilege are accepted as the norm, perpetuating raced hierarchies and maintaining barriers to equality. The narrative indicates responsibility to challenge whiteness in the process towards social justice in education by 'getting it right' in the early years (Ofsted, 2013). Change is more likely if there is understanding of the structures that reproduce racial hierarchies that disrupt the education of black children. In the analysis of Dawn's story, discussion of issues arising include anti-racist policy and practice; social policy and the impact on early years education; the need for communication within teams to hear diverse perspectives for effective policy implementation; and how personal and institutional whiteness impacts on the experiences of black children in the early years setting.

Dawn's day is represented through a fictional composite narrative in partial acceptance that stories told by white people cannot be from a position of racial realism, as racism is not a personal experience. Preston (2013, p. 2) suggests that white narratives represent the perspective of the 'unreliable narrator' who appreciates their limits when representing the black experience. In consideration of these limits, this story is drawn from a wide field including observations alongside discussions and interviews with black and white practitioners in the four schools and parents of the seven children in the project. Dawn is a composite character who represents genuine concern by all practitioners in the study to provide an inclusive environment. Her experiences may reflect those of many who are on the same journey in early years education. They are not intended to place blame but to indicate the influence of societal attitudes and the need to consider alternative ways of viewing positions on race and equality in the institutions within which we work. White people who are active in the battle against racism may have 'powerful desires' to push their whiteness away to disrupt the benefits accrued through the socially determined advantages in every aspect of their lives (Preston, 2013, p. 2). Dawn's story indicates opportunities to deny this powerful desire in the safe world of white privilege where challenges can be uncomfortable and discounted. Her story is in contrast to the counter-stories of the black children in this book that tell how, without addressing whiteness, processes towards social justice cannot be realised, leaving racism and its impact ever-present in their education.

Dawn's story

Dawn turns off the alarm clock as she wakes at the usual six thirty and turns over to cuddle her husband, John, who snores beside her. In a few minutes she will have to leave the comfort of her bed and start the morning routine that will lead to facing some difficult situations in school. As she relaxes in bed her thoughts gradually turn to the end of the previous school day. Dawn has been accused by an irate mother, Josephina, of doing nothing about the fact that her child, Pina, was racially abused by a boy in the playground. Josephina believes that incidents like this resulted in Pina cutting off large chunks of hair at home. Dawn discussed the incident with Josephina, which to her seemed just like children saying silly things to each other to get their own way. Anyway, how could she have done anything when Pina had said nothing? Pina always seems happy in the classroom and yesterday was no different. There must be another reason for her cutting her hair as, after all, 4-year-old children like to experiment with scissors – hadn't Peter (her own young son) once cut his sister's hair when they were making collage pictures together? What's the difference with Pina cutting her hair? John stirs next to her and looks at the clock. 'Time to get up' he grunts, shaking Dawn out of her thoughts. They both get out of bed and the morning routine begins.

Dawn's two children are washed and dressed and together they finish breakfast so that by seven thirty Dawn is ready to leave the house. She says goodbye, leaving John to make the children's packed lunches and ensure their school bags are ready. He does the school run, as his work hours are flexible but she always needs to be in school early to prepare the classroom and to attend meetings. School is only a fifteen-minute drive away as they had been able to move nearer when the children were born. She has been a teacher there for 6 years and she enjoys her job in the school, which has a multiracial intake with a wide cultural mix. She has learned so much about the children's different cultures by organising class projects such as Chinese New Year, Diwali and black history month. She was brought up in a rural community having very little contact with people from other cultures, so she is pleased that John persuaded her to move to the city when he was promoted. She enjoys the vibrancy of cultural diversity it offers, although their home is in a mainly white area just outside the school catchment.

As Dawn arrives at the school gate, she considers how she can best handle the incident with Pina. There won't be time to speak with Josephina in the morning as she is often in a rush to get to college, but she will have to find time after school as she can see Josephina is angry and won't let it drop. She must talk to Pina and find out what actually happened. Dawn enters the building and immediately confronts the responsibilities of the school day, not thinking about the incident again until Pina enters the classroom. She is surprised at Pina's appearance as her usually large '*afro*' is now neatly plaited. She compliments Pina on her new hairstyle. Pina smiles and joins her friend in the home play area. Dawn decides that she must find time to sit and speak with Pina alone in response to her mother's concerns and sees playtime as a good opportunity. She observes Pina during the morning happily joining in the activities and participating in the group session for phonics. There is no sign of distress, although she remembers when Pina had complained previously about children pulling and touching her hair a few times during group sessions. Children always fidget and touch each other when sitting in the group and she's always telling them to stop and concentrate, so she hadn't recognised at the time that Pina was upset.

It is playtime and Dawn asks Pina to stay in the classroom because she wants to speak with her. Pina stands silently, looking worried. When everyone has left the room, Dawn sits with Pina and tells her that Josephina was very cross yesterday and asks why she had cut her hair, upsetting her mother so much. Pina refuses to answer and after encouraging her unsuccessfully to discuss the incident, Dawn comments that anyway she has a '*nice new hairstyle now. It looks good in plaits*'. Pina stands ready to leave the room but Dawn stops her and asks what the boys in the playground had said. Pina looks anxious but is able to tell Dawn that they said she had the '*stupidest hair ever*' and wouldn't let her go on the climbing frame. Dawn is relieved to hear that the remark does not appear to be racist, as the consequences would be more serious and action would need to be taken. She comments that Pina shouldn't take any notice because children are often saying horrible things to each other when they can't get their own way. She asks Pina why she didn't tell anyone and Pina replies that she told Charmaine (a black practitioner) in the playground. Dawn brings the discussion to a close and Pina quickly runs outside to play.

Dawn uses the last five minutes of break to get a drink from the staffroom. As she enters, Charmaine is just leaving and Dawn asks her about the incident with Pina. Charmaine easily remembers and explains that the boy had insulted Pina's hair and she could understand why she was crying at the time because she knew how she felt. Dawn doesn't really understand Charmaine's comment, but recognising that it might be significant in her later discussions with Josephina asks if they could talk more at lunchtime. They agree to meet in the empty ICT room. As the morning progresses, Dawn notices that Pina is more subdued than earlier and sits for a long period quietly engaged in a cutting-out collage activity with her close friend. She doesn't participate in the whole class numeracy lesson, sitting quietly on the edge of the group. This concerns Dawn as it is uncharacteristic of Pina, who usually participates eagerly in the daily activity.

At the end of the morning Dawn meets with Charmaine to discuss the incident. As they eat their lunches together, Dawn begins the conversation by telling Charmaine that Pina's mother was very upset and she couldn't understand why, as young children often experiment with scissors, as had her own son. She is surprised at the intensity of Charmaine's reply:

> I'm not surprised that you don't understand because I bet no one has ever called your hair stupid! When you're black you often get insults about your hair! It's happened to me since I was young and I always wished my hair was straight and easy to manage like the white girls. It's only as I got older that I realised that my hair is not ugly like I was made to feel.

Dawn is silenced by the reply and avoids a response by asking why Charmaine had not told her about Pina being upset. Charmaine answers, recognising Dawn's uneasiness:

> I didn't see the point as nothing would be done – it never is, even though the policy said that racist incidents should be reported. It is only when someone is called a racist name that it is seen as hurtful so why say anything? It's just what black children have to get used to. They get their support from their home and their friends in school. Don't you notice how Pina always plays with Remmie in the playground? Black children learn to live alongside racism.

Dawn is surprised by Charmaine's words, as she hadn't perceived the comment as racist or understood racism as impacting in this way on black children's everyday lives. After another short silence, she asks Charmaine for advice on how she can deal with the situation and in particular what she should say to Josephina that evening. Charmaine suggests that Dawn think more about how black children experience racism and how this is addressed in school. She advises her to speak more with Pina but not to single her out in the way she had at playtime, as it might make her feel more of a victim than give her the support she needs. She suggests that an additional help may be to provide a beauty parlour in the reception imaginative play area for a while. This could raise discussion with all the children about attitudes to difference in appearance rather than only with those children involved in the incident. As for meeting with Josephina, Dawn herself would have to decide on how to approach that discussion.

It is the end of lunchtime and Dawn thanks Charmaine for opening her eyes to how Pina was feeling and acknowledges how useful it would be to have more team discussions with black colleagues who have such experiences. As she returns to the classroom she thinks about her approach to the situation that day and why she was unsettled by the intensity of Charmaine's responses at lunchtime. It opened her eyes to the fact that she had not considered the situation from Pina's or Josephina's perspectives and, not having experienced racism personally, had only seen the significance from her own position. She had heard racist comments when she was growing up and was told by her parents how bad they were. She knew then that racism was wrong but without really understanding the emotional significance to those on the receiving end. Dawn spent the rest of the afternoon carrying out her classroom duties as usual but with her mind preoccupied with the events of the morning. When Josephina arrives, she calls her to one side and apologises for not considering the incident with the seriousness it deserves and says that although she had spoken to Pina she understands that this is not enough and she will think of better ways to address such situations when they arise. Josephina does not seem satisfied and asks to meet Dawn in the near future to discuss further action taken in the school, as *'these kinds of comments are very upsetting and shouldn't happen again'*. After school Dawn makes an appointment with the head teacher to reflect on the day's events, as she feels she needs to better understand her reactions to what Charmaine has said and discuss how to better support black children.

When she gets home, after they finish dinner and put the children to bed, Dawn sits down with John to relax and she recounts the day's events. She is relieved, as he makes her feel better, especially when he retorts: *'But that's not racist!'* regarding the boy's comment to Pina. *'Perhaps everyone is overreacting'* she replies as they go to bed.

Reflections on Dawn's story

Gaps between the experiences of white practitioners and black children

Dawn's story indicates aspects of white privilege that mark the social divide between many practitioners and some of their black pupils. These differences in life chances and social and economic experiences make it difficult for those practitioners to understand out-of-school factors impinging on black children's education. Dawn's home, on the outskirts of a multicultural urban town, is reflective of many white middle-class teachers. This may be a choice that many black families do not have, partly due to racism in rented housing policy, mortgage availability, and employment among other structural factors in society, contributing to social exclusion (MacGregor-Smith, 2017). Sometimes it can be a choice, as it may be safer to live within and belong to a supportive community that reflects the family's identity rather than be exposed regularly to racism and feelings of being an outsider (BBC, 2018). The resulting socio-economic position of many black families and the pressures placed on them when they strive to secure well-paid careers can cause added stress and increased health problems. Dawn's life is contextualised by economic and social conditions offered through white privilege, free of the discriminatory and emotionally charged aspects of racism (Frankenberg, 2009). Her easy, relatively stress-free morning routine differs from that of Pina's family. Josephina's stress is compounded by Pina cutting her hair, alongside her habitual concerns to get three children to school and be on time for college. Unlike Dawn, this is without the support of her partner, who no longer lives with the family. More overt issues of race have also impacted on Josephina's day through the distress of racism in school having an emotional effect on Pina. The commonality of socially determined factors that induce stress is also present in the experiences of other families in this study. Some black parents spoke of unemployment and worrying economic situations, substandard housing and personal family circumstances as integral to their lives in addition to that of the usual responsibilities of family life. Practitioners can be unaware of socio-economic factors in context with black children's experiences in school. This may leave aspects of social disadvantage interpreted through deficit models of black families and racialised stereotypes such as lateness, disorganisation and lack of care (Bradbury, 2013). Middle-class, professional families in the research of Rollock et al. (2015, p. 101) tell how they are stereotyped as being working class with a racialised identity prioritising a classed identity. There is often a lack of opportunity for building trusting, supportive relationships with parents to understand their home circumstances. Misinterpretations can prevent appropriate support being offered and perpetuate stereotypes of disadvantage based on racialised assumptions, impacting on children's experiences in early years education.

Events of the previous day have introduced the realities of racism into Dawn's life, disturbing her morning routine as she reflects on them. However, her subjectivity of whiteness enables her more easily to dismiss thoughts of racism. She finds it difficult to identify with such problems in context with her own personal material and emotional experiences. She is able to proceed without them interrupting her morning routine. Processes of whiteness have evolved as normative in British society to determine a hierarchy built on subordination of other racialised and classed social groups (Preston, 2013). Practitioners can be unaware of their own positions in establishing whiteness and hierarchies of power that discriminate and marginalise children whose cultural experiences differ from their accepted norm. Colour-blind approaches to difference can be a barrier to recognition of how whiteness reproduces inequalities, whereas discussions of racism may disrupt a common conception of whiteness as a 'culture of niceness' (McIntyre, 1997, p. 46). Colour-blindness can also be a way to protect white communities from thoughts and practices that may challenge white privilege through acknowledgement and subsequent action. During discussions with white practitioners the subject of racism is often diverted to gender, as this aspect of inequality is easier to relate to personally and therefore understand. This shift to the paradigm of gender inequality also avoids confrontation with attitudes to race by identifying action within what is perceived as a less threatening and contentious issue. Dismissal of racism as a problem can reaffirm whiteness as a culture of niceness. Through denial of racism in her privileged position as a white professional, Dawn can continue her life materially advantaged by racism, whereas Pina's family and Charmaine continue to live with the consequences as a daily reality.

Colour-blind denial of race and racism

The English government's low priority on addressing race equality (Chapter 7) has resulted in marginalising action to challenge the racialisation of pupils. As a consequence, there are few opportunities for teams to reach consensus on what constitutes a racist incident so that only clearly overt abuse may be recognised. This is highlighted by Dawn's interpretation of Pina's experience in the playground and the psychological impact that it may have had. Racial micro-aggressions such as this can easily go unreported without clear understanding of what is a racist incident, as demonstrated through Charmaine's belief that *'nothing would be done'*. Mirza (2004, p. 206) proposes that some black women teachers avoid the subject of racism when working in a white school ethos, partly in recognition of resistance to action within existing institutional power structures. Charmaine feels more able to voice her views when her white colleague brings up the subject of racism. A reason for her previous lack of action against Pina's incident may have been because of a colour-blind ethos in the school that she feels she can now challenge in her discussions with Dawn.

Despite some action being taken against racism, this can be superficial with schools being an integral aspect of the social system. Schools are likely to reproduce existing racialised structures in society through prioritising external demands and monitoring, thus 'reinforcing and reproducing the status quo' (Banks, 2006, p. 210). Although this may occur at macro level, changes implemented to challenge inequalities can make a difference at micro level to children's experiences of racialisation. However, action in response to the Race Relations Act (2000) and resulting race equality policies has had little impact as practitioners may interpret race equality through an uncritical multicultural pedagogy (see Chapter 7). Later in Dawn's day colour-blindness is indicated through her decision that action could be an indication of a lack of proportion given to meanings of racism. There is a belief that young children are not sophisticated enough in their thinking to actively engage in complex racial ideas to manipulate their social standing in play situations (Hart, 2009). Incidents of racism are then blamed on other factors such as mimetic behaviour, where children are merely repeating comments and ideas that they have heard without understanding. Strategic colour-blindness can avoid discussion, placing blame on those abused for misinterpreting comments (Dent, 2009, p. 26). Young children are capable of using racist language whether consciously or unconsciously, intentionally or unintentionally in their interactions with peers. A familiar colour-blind response to accusations of racism is to regard them as an overreaction to an incident or as an imagined situation. Where black children remain unsupported in the face of the psychological effects of racial micro-aggressions, this can imply that the white abusers are accepted as more dominant in the classroom, conveying a sense of powerlessness and marginalisation for those abused (Hill et al., 2007). During the research period, a practitioner is present when the children are queuing to leave the classroom. One of only two white boys standing in the queue offends a black boy to the point of tears by calling him *'chocolate face*'. The term used is based on a common form of racial micro-assault learned by the white child who uses it consciously in this situation to offend his black peer. Despite being a minority in the class, he is confident using his whiteness as a form of power in a large group of black children. The practitioner does not respond while the black boy shows increasing distress. When the researcher discusses the incident with her, she dismisses it by saying that it is a term heard on a TV advert for chocolate and '*no harm is meant*'. The statement indicates a naive approach to implications of racism. Colour-blindness reinforces hierarchies of whiteness as the norm in social relationships. Blame is placed on the black child for being upset, as colour-blindness enables her to interpret the comment as insignificant. She may be using it strategically to avoid confronting the incident with the children who are aware of racialised attitudes and stereotypes in the media. Colour-blindness can result in practitioners not acknowledging that young children either understand or experience racism, therefore not seeing it as developmentally appropriate to raise these issues with them. However, if opportunities are not afforded to discuss rather than ignore these incidents, they can result in repeated psychologically damaging racial micro-aggressions. The white class teacher also seems unsure of how to address the incident when informed later by the researcher. She has noticed '*that this is going on*' between the children and '*must do something about it*' but has not discussed strategies with colleagues. No further action was taken to address the incident or to support the boy who experienced the intentional micro-assault. Absence of action implies approval of the white child's remarks, leaving all those present exposed to an accepted racialised hierarchy of the minority white children. Lack of understanding and confidence to challenge this situation indicates the need for a whole team approach and consensus regarding meanings and implications of racism. Policy can then be established and consistent action determined towards ensuring an institutional ethos in which all forms of racism are acknowledged, discussed openly and managed effectively (Chapter 8).

The importance of hearing counter-stories when forming policy and action to address racism

Dawn's discussion with Charmaine opens up issues that challenge her understandings of the impact of racism on Pina. Subsequently, when away from the situation in the comfort of her home, these issues are easily abated by Dawn through consciously blocking the realities of racism. Dawn approaches the head teacher alone for further discussion, perhaps to support an understanding from another, less challenging, white perspective. Alternatively, excluding Charmaine may be because she feels her presence a threat to her whiteness and her own attitudes to race. Meeting alone with the head teacher will not challenge established hierarchies of power in the school and any subsequent action could be made through institutional norms. By meeting alone they are not including or understanding racism through Charmaine's direct experience. This omission can enable Dawn to reduce her anxiety and diminish the emotional effects of marginalisation and exclusion that then become secondary in decisions made for future action. Without in-depth understanding of how racism is reproduced from perspectives of those who experience it, there can be difficulty in development of substantial, strategic anti-racist policy. Any further action may be tokenistic without addressing more covert ways in which children are racialised through the hidden curriculum and school ethos of whiteness. Charmaine indicates familiarity with white denial and the strategies used to avoid addressing racism by not advising Dawn about her approach to Josephina, emphasising that it should come from Dawn herself. This can encourage Dawn's self-reflection on the issues that they discussed together. Practitioners in the study voiced the importance of talking to black colleagues as a way of understanding different approaches to race and racism and how personal attitudes may impact on the education of black children.

Black pupils have been found to prefer and relate better to black teachers, feeling that they are treated more fairly than by white staff who may assign negative stereotypes to them (Tatum, 2005). Because of their own experiences of institutional and personal racialisation, black staff can directly influence classroom practice as well as policy and procedure. Dialogue between practitioners, such as that of Dawn and Charmaine, can create an ethos in which positive, thoughtful action can be taken and evaluated to challenge barriers between staff and pupils. Parents should also be involved in this process as in two of the schools in the project. A regular discussion group takes place in one school between parents and staff to address racism between the many diverse cultural groups in the school. The group was initially formed in response to a racist incident between parents in the playground and has evolved to inform strategic anti-racist policy and practice. In a second school a voluntary funded project provides a safe place for parents and staff to discuss their concerns. A black parent attended regular sessions to discuss conflict in the school regarding use of a term that was unacceptable in the school but not in the child's home. These initiatives can be helpful in supporting critical anti-racist practice that challenges perspectives derived from white cultural norms. In Josephina's situation, her distress could have been mitigated if she had the opportunity to speak to someone able to understand and support her concern over Pina's experiences of racism; similarly, this would address Charmaine's lack of confidence in race equality policy.

The perils of a non-critical multicultural education

Multiculturalism is discussed in Chapter 7 as framing national and local equality policy at macro level in *EYFS* guidance in England. Dawn indicates an interpretation of inclusion through a cultural pluralist model. Although this model promotes equality through celebrating, valuing and learning about other socio-cultural experiences, this occurs primarily through essentialised stereotypes of religious and cultural celebrations. Planning celebrations in isolation of the mainstream curriculum marginalises children's cultures by exoticising them and polarising difference in relation to commonly accepted norms of British culture. Those topics represented through food, music and artefacts can then assign cultural stereotypes to groups identified through religious affinities alongside racialised and generalised characteristics such as Chinese, Asian and African. Such concepts do not include the many cultural nuances and are reinforced through notions of assimilation and the 'melting pot' concept of British culture. These stereotypes often guide race equality policy formulation outside a critical, reflexive framework. The multicultural curriculum can therefore be interpreted to maintain rather than challenge dominant white power relations through marginalisation of the history and cultures of the black students (Ladson-Billings, 2009). This approach is apparent in EYFS curriculum guidance, where suggestions are made to incorporate diverse cultures through resources and celebrations of festivals to support children from 'ethnic minority' communities (DfE, 2017). Dawn views such celebrations as beneficial to her understanding of diversity without including them in the general complexities of British culture through curriculum design. Charmaine advises Dawn to organise the environment to facilitate discussion with the children regarding difference and to challenge accepted norms – in this case those related to hierarchies of physical appearance. Charmaine's own experiences of racism contribute to her realisation of the need for a critical pedagogy which challenges negative attitudes rather than colour-blind denial of the need to raise issues of race and racism. Her suggestion of a beauty parlour resourced for role play can contribute diverse approaches to haircare during children's conceptual exploration for new knowledge. This enables children to build on socio-cultural experiences rather than isolate them from their learning by compartmentalising important aspects of their identity.

Dawn struggles to find time during the day to speak with Pina, and the short time in which they meet gives little opportunity for Pina to voice her feelings. The fact that Pina misses playtime and is alone in the classroom could further intimidate her into silence. Time for listening to children is increasingly limited as practitioners are involved in meeting developmental targets as a result of a pedagogic culture of accountability and curriculum management. Current child-centred pedagogy is primarily concerned with interactions related to developmental outcomes, which limits engagement with the intersectional implications of sexism and racism in children's words or actions (Campbell, 2005). Although the children in this study are allowed some time during the day for self-directed play, practitioners recounted the limits imposed on this by government initiatives such as phonics teaching. The time available each day for play enables children to represent their personal experiences through self-directed activity free of interactions planned to meet predetermined curriculum objectives. During play sessions children use strategies to support transition from home to the school culture whilst maintaining their primary identities and building on preschool experiences to explore new opportunities for learning. This is evident in the pattie making in Pina's café (Chapter 5) and Devon's forest play (Chapter 3). Imaginative play is essential for children to make sense of their worlds and represent their experiences in order to further an understanding of their identity in society. They are able to tell their stories through their play through both action and language. Playful pedagogy can also give practitioners opportunities for observation and so give them opportunities to understand how children are representing personal interpretations and emotions through their activity. It can also allow time to interact with children to critically discuss issues in the context of their activity. Charmaine's suggestion of a beauty parlour can allow Pina to represent her thoughts about her hair and give Dawn an opportunity to observe and discuss the implications of the micro-aggression in a non-threatening situation. For Louis (Chapter 4), playing with the garage gives insight into cultural norms and activity outside the school where he spends a lot of time with his father, who is a mechanic. His play with small cars can be extended to outdoor play through resources for garage role play to include a similar experience for other children. Opportunities for children to discuss feelings in line with cultural representations will enable practitioners to raise issues and extend learning in context with their activity. Realities of young children's diverse experiences are then incorporated into general curriculum provision. Learning becomes more meaningful and relevant, rather than detached through a non-critical multiculturalism. Critical multiculturalism can support children to challenge racialisation when attitudes to race are discussed with practitioners in connection with their everyday experiences in the setting. Children who voice negative attitudes through play can also be supported to recognise disadvantages and harm to themselves and others.

Black children's representations of self in the early years classroom

Dawn's thoughts about overreactions to the situation can deny the drip-drip effects of everyday micro-aggressions and the psychological impact on those who are othered. The stories in this book reveal how practitioners may remain unaware of how black children experience race and racism and how the hidden curriculum contributes to the silencing of their voices. Pina's experiences of racism can be interpreted through the action of cutting her hair that calls for recognition of her emotional reaction to the micro-assaults against her. Dawn silences Pina's voice through initial denial of both the seriousness of the incident and the effect it may have on her. Pina's reactions are better understood by Josephina and Charmaine from their similar experiences of racialisation. It is possible for Dawn to minimise the severity of Pina's pain by relating her actions to developmental stages. For example, Dawn rationalises Pina's action as a phase in development of cutting various materials when learning to use scissors. Her biography prevents her from grasping the experience of the black child, as she interprets Pina's use of scissors through the actions of her own white child, who does not have the same exposure to racism. Pina's experiences represent those of other children in this study who are faced daily with a conflict of what is acceptable in their homes and communities in contrast with values and expectations in school.

To conform to the expectation of being good learners, children may develop double-consciousness. Both Delgado (2000) and DuBois (2009) suggest that this can be psychologically damaging to children as they attempt to maintain a strong black identity to survive in a privileged white world. Thompson (2014) refers to this as the acquisition of a proxy identity, formed through a need to hide their true selves to conform to expectations in school and as a necessary tool in a racialised society. A proxy identity can be related to the intersections of race and class in the use of home dialects that represent both aspects of identity. The middle-class dialect of English in the school is accepted as the institutional norm and is often unfamiliar as they start school. Children are expected to become bi- or multi-dialectical as well as conforming to other new cultural norms. Perhaps to support them through this process, four of the black boys in this study formed close friend-ships with white boys who appeared to accept their true selves and with whom they could share common socio-cultural experiences. Through these relationships the need for a proxy identity is to some extent dissipated, as the children under-stand an identity as black British that incorporates elements of the home culture with that of the school. Jason has a friendship with a white boy that supports him to manage classroom norms while remaining confident to express his black iden-tity. Examples of this are through role play as a black superhero in the playground, and an occasion when he challenges a stereotype of black boys assigned to him by a practitioner (Chapter 3). Same-race friendships are also important in maintain-ing a black identity, as is indicated through the stories of Pina, Sonic, Kylie and Devon, all of whom have formed those friendships alongside relationships with peers of different cultures and racialised identities. Devon's story indicates the importance of cultural identification, as he is comfortable using patois when with Neil. His confidence to rap with Alan indicates a sense of security gained from his friendship with Neil, while affirming his identity with his white friend. This is not so for either Pina or Jason, who use patois only when alone and unheard. Their actions reveal an understanding of their cultural identities being environ-mentally marginalised and inappropriate in the classroom culture. Barley (2013, p. 187) sees language and identity as closely intertwined, with language being an important 'symbolic marker of identity'. Her research emphasises the importance of playful pedagogies that give young children opportunities to use home lan-guages and dialects. Marginalisation of dialect variation in spoken English can be reproduced through the hidden curriculum. For example, the emphasis on stan-dardised English in the phonics method of literacy teaching can exclude dialects through phonetic pronunciation. This approach contributes to the racialisation of identities through the hierarchy of an accepted pronunciation in spoken English. This can result in a need to suppress dialects to be accepted in British society, often perceived as necessary to achieve in education and employment (Blackman, 2017). The resulting invisibility of cultural nuances becomes an element of double-consciousness. The bicultural competences of the children gained through friend-ships and opportunities to express black identities have given children in this study confidence to challenge their racialisation. They adapt to the school culture and maintain their identities through positive interactions rather than through behav-iours that negatively challenge classroom norms and are interpreted as disruptive.

Summary – what can be learned from the white voice?

Dawn's story emphasises that change cannot come through a colour-blind ideology that reproduces the hierarchies of whiteness and privilege. Black children will continue to be disadvantaged through a positioning of whiteness as the norm if action is not taken to address racialisation through institutional and interactional practices. Better progress can be made towards a common aim of equality by understanding how and why whiteness is constructed and maintained. Black children can then be supported to challenge micro-aggressions and stereotypes that impact on their dispositions to learning as well as their emotional well-being. They can explore new knowledge through a curriculum that builds on familiar concepts and cultural perspectives.

Three important issues can be drawn from Dawn's story in the challenge to whiteness and the racialisation of black children in the early years setting:

* There is a need to understand both covert and overt processes that racialise black children in order to address the impact on their identity as learners.
* Understanding race and racism, as well as consensus in the meaning of these terms, is necessary to challenge racialisation through institutional practices and procedures. This is important for effective implementation of race equality policy.
* A critical, reflexive pedagogy inclusive of black children's socio-cultural experiences and knowledge is crucial. This must also offer opportunities for reflection on processes of whiteness, including how personal perspectives influence practice.

As emphasised in CRT, it is not enough to theorise about issues discussed in this book, as action must be taken to challenge the racialisation of black children from the beginning of their education. Chapter 8 suggests ways that this can be done through an institutional culture that recognises and encourages meaningful discussion of racism. Subsequent action underpinned by a theoretical lens can enable progress towards social justice in early years settings.

Reflective practice

* Gain a consensus through discussion with colleagues on interpretations of what is unacceptable language and behaviour. This can ensure consistent policy implementation to support black children when abused and can help the perpetrators to understand the implications on themselves and others at personal and societal levels.
* Be prepared to address incidents when they occur to ensure the abused child is supported and any racialised hierarchy that exists within the peer group is challenged.

References

Banks, J. A. (2006) *Race, Culture and Education: The Selected Works of J.A. Banks*. Oxon: Routledge.

Barley, R. (2013) *An Anthropological Exploration of Identity and Social Interaction in a Multi-Ethnic Classroom*. Unpublished doctoral thesis: Sheffield Hallam University, Sheffield, UK.

BBC (2018) *Stephen: The Murder That Changed a Nation S01E031*. London: On the Corner/ Rogan Productions for the BBC. Available on UTube. Accessed 2 July 2018.

Blackman, M. (2017) *BBC Word of Mouth Podcast – 19.09.17*. Available from BBC iPlayer. Accessed 10 January 2018.

Bradbury, A. (2013) *Understanding Early Years Inequality: Policy, Assessment and Young Children's Identities*. Oxon: Routledge.

Campbell, S. (2005) Secret Children's Business, in Yelland, N. (ed.), *Critical Issues in Early Childhood Education*. Berkshire: Open University Press.

Delgado, R. (2000) Storytelling for Oppositionists and Others: A Plea for Narrative, in Delgado, R. and Stefancic, J. (eds.), *Critical Race Theory: The Cutting Edge*, 2nd ed. Philadelphia, USA: Temple University Press.

Dent, D. (2009) 'I Don't See Colour': Race Equality and Strategic Colour Blindness in Schools, in *Race Equality Teaching*, 28 (1) pp. 25–30.

DfE (2017) *Early Years Foundation Stage Profile Handbook*. London: Her Majesty's Stationary Office.

DuBois, W. E. B. (2009) The Conservation of Races, in Back, L. and Solomos, J. (eds.), *Theories of Race and Racism, a Reader*, 2nd ed. Oxon: Routledge.

Frankenberg, R. (2009) White Women, Race Matters, in Back, L. and Solomos, J. (eds.), *Theories of Race and Racism, a Reader*, 2nd ed. Oxon: Routledge.

Hart, I. (2009) *The Myth of Racist Kids*. London: Manifesto Club.

Hill, M., Graham, C., Caulfield, C., Ross, N. and Shelton, A. (2007) Interethnic Relations among Children in School: The Perspectives of Young People in Scotland, in *European Journal of Education*, 42 (2) pp. 267–279.

Ladson-Billings, G. (2009) Just What Is CRT and What's It Doing in a Nice Field Like Education, in Taylor, E., Gillborn, D. and Ladson-Billings, G. (eds.), *Foundations of Critical Race Theory in Education*. Oxon: Routledge.

MacGregor-Smith, R. (2017) *Race in the Workplace, the MacGregor-Smith Review*. Available from www.gov.uk>publications>race-in-the-workplace. Accessed 10 October 2017.

McIntyre, A. (1997) *Making Meaning of Whiteness: Exploring Racial Identity with White Teachers*. New York, USA: State University of New York Press.

Mirza, H. S. (2004) Black Women in Education, in Ladson-Billings, G. and Gillborn, D. (eds.), *Multicultural Education*. London: Routledge Falmer.

Office for Standards in Education (OFSTED) (2013) *Getting It Right First Time: Achieving and Maintaining High-Quality Early Years Provision*. Available from www.ofsted.gov.uk/ resources/130117. Accessed 7 July 2017.

Preston, J. (2013) *Whiteness in Academia: Counter-Stories of Betrayal and Resistance*. Newcastle upon Tyne: Cambridge Scholars Publishing.

Rollock, N., et al. (2015) *The Colour of Class*. Oxon: Routledge.

Tatum, A. W. (2005) *Teaching Reading to Black Adolescent Males: Closing the Achievement Gap*. Maine, USA: Stenhouse Publishers.

Thompson, L. (2014) Keynote Lecture: True and False Self and Proxy Identities in Black and Minority Ethnic Children, in *Proceedings of the Seminar Thinking Spaces, July 3 2014, London*. Tavistock and Portman NHS Foundation Trust, Swiss Cottage, London.

7

PLAY AND MULTICULTURALISM

Some relevant debates and issues

Introduction

To contextualise the children's stories and the positions of parents and practitioners in this study, this chapter includes discussion on factors that influence a commitment to provide an inclusive early years environment. The four primary schools that the children attend see equality of opportunity as a priority for management and classroom practice. Practitioners view diversity as valuable in the education and care of all children in multicultural Britain. However, current English government priorities in education have prevented a focus on equality action as training budgets are redirected to support a managerial pedagogy to meet measured attainment targets. Emphasis on achievement in OfSTED inspections has resulted in a low priority on monitoring race equality. Since revised legislation in the Equalities Act (2006), inspectors prioritise aspects of the broader inclusive equalities agenda, further marginalising race equality policy. Although race is included as an element in discrimination, there is no longer a focus on racism as a major contributor to inequality in the same way as in previous documents. Race is now subsumed under the general equality duties of the Equality and Human Rights Commission (EHRC).

The first part of this chapter discusses how play can support the education of black children and the reasons why it has been recently questioned as being appropriate in current emphasis on achievement through measured targets. Play has been central to good early years practice through advocates such as Froebel, Isaacs, Montessori, Bruner, Piaget and Vygotsky. The Curriculum Guidance (DfE, 2017a, p. 9) recognises child-led play as 'essential for children's development' when guided by their emerging needs and interests and supported through skilled adult interaction. The children's stories in this book indicate the importance of play through cultural representations that are not always possible through a more formal pedagogy. However, data indicates that black children in secondary education disproportionally underachieve in the education system (Gillborn, 2016). These statistics give parents concern for their children's future opportunities in society. A formal early years pedagogy is viewed by some black parents as directly related to high achievement rather than one based on play (Sillin, 2005; Brooker, 2010). An emphasis on achievement in basic subjects can be interpreted as particularly necessary for black children to gain access to qualifications in recognition of racial discrimination in society being a barrier to life chances (MacGregor-Smith, 2017). Rather than from prescribed outcomes with little relevance to young children, learning through play is from a starting point of their individual stages in development, interests, personal identities and experiences. Play can give opportunities for independent exploration, creating a positive foundation for motivation to learn and future educational success.

Since the 1970s multicultural education has been a strategy to ensure equal access to the early years curriculum and a means to celebrate and include the diverse cultural heritages of young black British children. The second part of this chapter discusses if multicultural education is an appropriate strategy to address inequalities in early years education. Although celebrations and languages of children's home cultures have been commonly included in the curriculum, multicultural education has been challenged as a Eurocentric approach that may omit histories, general content and experiences relevant to black children (Guishard-Pine, 2010). Within an inclusive pedagogy there is need for meaningful communication between parents and practitioners to bridge cultural gaps between home and school to provide an appropriate and supportive learning environment. This chapter argues that both play and multiculturalism can be effective within a critical framework that acts against the processes that contribute to the racialisation of black children. Listening to the perspectives of parents and carers through effective partnerships is essential to this process. Action can then be taken to address their concerns to ensure a more inclusive and relevant education for all children in early years settings.

The relevance of play to black children's early years education

Self-directed play that allows opportunities to explore and learn according to individual development and personal experiences has been the foundation upon which early years pedagogy has developed in Britain since the early twentieth century. The Plowden Report (CACE, 1967) formally introduced play as the accepted pedagogy in early years education. More recent affirmation has been through research in the Effective Provision of Preschool Education Project (EPPE, 2004) and the Cambridge Primary Review (2009). Social interaction between peers and practitioners during play is an essential element in the acquisition of new knowledge, beliefs and behaviours. Play can give opportunities to share cultural knowledge and practices during the construction of new meanings, dispositions and identities (Rogoff, 2003). The children's stories in this book indicate the value of play for opportunities to express their identities and experiences when adapting to the new school culture. Through play new knowledge is acquired by building on that previously gained from experiences in the home. Social and emotional development is supported during play by interactions in the micro-social world of the early years setting, enabling children to function in wider society. Play in the outside environment of the setting supports physical development; these opportunities are becoming increasingly difficult for those living in urban areas. Most importantly, play contextualises children's past and present experiences, enabling them to link their understandings holistically as they are ready to further develop and learn. The children's stories tell of how cultural meanings are given to new situations to problem-solve (Devon); acquire maths (Pina) and literacy (Sonic) concepts; use imagination to understand emotions (Jason); and develop social skills (Kylie and Shania). By determining and developing self-directed activity during play, children can apply cultural knowledge and experiences from home to those new to them, enhancing their learning and development. Vygotsky (1986) proposed that the impact of the individual child's external social world should be acknowledged as crucial to their education. Learning cannot be seen in isolation of events in their individual worlds. A socio-cultural pedagogy allows for home experiences to connect with institutional traditions. Play provides opportunities to involve common socio-cultural meanings shared with peers in the classroom context, while allowing unique cultural experiences to contribute to children's activities. This is particularly apparent through the stories of Devon (Chapter 3), Sonic (Chapter 4) and Pina (Chapter 5) as they share cultural meanings during their imaginative play.

The importance of interventions in play to support black children

It is important for practitioners to observe play and intervene when necessary as children may use their agency to disrupt the many benefits (Van Ausdale and Feagin, 2001). As groups of children dominate learning contexts, play can sometimes prevent the expression of home cultures (Broadhead and Burt, 2012). Play can also be used by children to reinforce gendered and racialised hierarchies understood by them from experiences in wider society. Although turn-taking rules aim to provide access to resources, this may deny some children opportunities to play. Children may use the power relationships of whiteness and designated genders to negotiate access to the play by intentionally breaking the set boundaries (Campbell, 2005). By expecting rules alone to provide equality of access for all children, these occasions can go unchallenged without awareness of racialised and gendered dynamics. Negotiation for resources can also go uncontested by the excluded children, who may see privilege in the classroom as the norm, mirroring dominant hierarchies in society. As children conform to expectations of belonging by adopting new cultural meanings, they may the need to conceal their cultural identities to prevent exclusion from the dominance of whiteness as the norm. This is representative of double-consciousness, discussed in Chapter 2, as psychological support for black children as they navigate their place in racialised hierarchies. The following narrative of a black child excluded from a close friendship indicates an awareness of the hierarchy of whiteness and his experience of racialisation as an outsider. He tells his mother that he does not want to be brown anymore because a girl he likes may not be his friend as she prefers to play with white boys. Although the girl has not made any overt remarks regarding racial preferences, the boy interpreted her preferences from attitudes towards race that he has understood as prevalent in society and conveyed unintentionally through play (Robinson and Jones Diaz, 2006). All young children need opportunities to discuss their feelings and attitudes regarding race and diversity to understand implications for themselves and others during their early experiences of socialisation. These situations emphasise the importance of early adult interventions in play to support independent challenges to racialised perceptions as children mature and become more articulate and able to self-manage their social relationships. Education may marginalise black children if not framed by an understanding of the diverse socio-cultural experiences and perspectives from which children approach the early years environment. Child-centred pedagogy is an effective approach to link personal experiences to knowledge and development but it can also ignore the relationship of education with society (Giroux, 1997, 2009). MacNaughton points out that play must be supported through critical intervention to prevent any negative psychological impact.

> Play can be where others hurt you, call you names, ignore your ideas and exclude you. . . . When children of colour play with white children . . . play can be risky. . . . If this is the case, then non-interference enables racism and sexism to continue.
>
> *(2003, p. 58)*

This statement emphasises the importance of a critical pedagogy that recognises the existence and implications of racism in children's lives to understand when to intervene in play to address such situations. This is possible by understanding the covert ways in which social relationships are manipulated through racialised hierarchies and stereotyped notions of others. Play can reveal young children's interpretations of their identities in relation to those of others to inform a critical practice. Children's attitudes can then be questioned and challenged as they emerge to enhance the benefits of play for all children. When supported by practitioners through a critical pedagogy, the experiences gained through play can give black children confidence to assert their identities by challenging their racialisation, taking positive action towards future goals in their education.

Challenges to playful pedagogy in early years education

A culture of 'school readiness' has challenged interpretations of play, replacing child-determined activities with those designed by adults to meet prescribed developmental and learning outcomes (McDowall Clark, 2017, p. 122). The current EYFS guidance demands a balance of adult-directed and child-led play. In reception classes, the guidance requires more time spent on planned teaching rather than play to help children prepare for more formal learning to be ready for Year 1 (DfE, 2017a). In response, activity is more frequently directed by adults to conform to assessment levels and wider expectations of schooling through accountable, prescribed objectives (Chapter 4). These demands have resulted in a more didactic pedagogy that precludes time for play opportunities where children can use their agency to adjust to the new culture of the school community. Conflict and anxiety can be a consequence for young black children as they adopt newly racialised identities without adequate opportunities to express their emotions and thoughts in the essentially white world of the classroom. Black boys in particular can be labelled as being disruptive through unacceptable behaviour when they initially attempt to adjust to the reception classroom culture (Bradbury, 2013). This is particularly apparent during whole class teaching sessions that take time away from opportunities to learn through play. Reasons given for their unacceptable behaviour are given based on 'discourses of poor parenting, single-motherhood, violence and neediness' without acknowledgement of cultural conflicts resulting from unfamiliar school norms (Bradbury, 2013, p. 112). Managerial pedagogy minimises opportunities for practitioners to observe children and challenge interpretations of their activity that can stereotype them as bad learners through preformed racialised identities and cultures. Education policy based on cultural uniformity and a transmission model relies on the teaching of narrow curricula rather than allowing for a broad perspective through playful activity (Giroux, 2009). Adult-led activity focused on specific objectives can prevent rather than encourage critical thinking, as aims are predetermined rather than arising from sequential consequences and observation of children's action. A transmission model can be related to revisions in the EYFS statutory framework (DfE, 2017a) such as assessment through the phonics-based screening test and is likely to result in prescribed teaching methods. Didactic approaches may discourage reading for pleasure, critique and lifelong learning as they disregard different learning styles, prior knowledge, interests and cultural experiences of children. Phonics teaching can also marginalise children's home languages and dialects as assessments standardise articulation of the English language. A consequential denial of dialects presumes hierarchical cultural uniformity, negatively reinforcing ideas of otherness based on the intersections of race, class and national identity. Emerging pedagogies based on such narrow developmental norms may produce a regime of truth that reproduces inequalities in education through a managerial rather than an ethical frame (Lea, 2014). Alternatively, playful pedagogies enable children to find an identity of being black and British by expressing and building on their cultural experiences in the new environment of the early years setting.

Although play as a pedagogical tool has dominated British educational philosophy, guiding early years curriculum for decades, this is not the same for all cultures. Preferences of some black parents are for more traditional methods of education. Wood (2010, p. 20) found that some from 'ethnic minority groups' hold contrasting expectations of schooling to that of practitioners, including both their understandings of play-based approaches as well as relationships between children and adults.

Cultural differences can create tensions between parents and practitioners, leading to mistrust and misunderstandings, as parents may feel that their children are not being taught appropriately. One reason for this may be widely reported performance data indicating underachievement of black children. A pedagogy that focuses on academic subjects measured through attainment targets can be viewed by parents as tangible evidence that their children are being supported to gain qualifications essential for future employment in a competitive society, where racism in recruitment practices discriminates against black applicants. It is important for practitioners to understand these concerns and ensure that these are discussed to address any concerns that a playful pedagogy is contributing to a lack of achievement. Play offers a foundation for future learning as it enables children to transfer knowledge to different contexts as they experience new situations and tackle new problems (McDowall Clark, 2017, p. 28). Practitioners can discuss with parents the stories of their children, such as those in this book, to communicate how targets in the early years curriculum are met through play. Formal and informal meetings with practitioners to share their children's achievement through observations; books and displays of children's learning journeys; and representations through photos, videos or children's art can inform parents of their children's learning through play. Developing technologies can be additional aids to sharing information alongside responsibilities for issues of security and confidentiality. These ways of communicating can support parents to be secure in the knowledge that their children are receiving support for their education by meeting curriculum targets through their play, and that their cultural knowledge is applied to their learning.

Opportunities for parents to discuss how their children are learning through play can impart an understanding of the lifelong benefits that play can offer through conceptual understanding rather than more formal didactic teaching, which has less lasting meaning for young children.

Multicultural education: inclusion or exclusion?

Multicultural education evolved in the USA as a response to the work of civil rights activists in the 1950s and 1960s. The civil rights movement demanded a curriculum relevant to all pupils, challenging overt discrimination apparent in the education system. It was introduced into Britain in the late 1970s during a shift in social policy from cultural assimilation to integration and cultural pluralism (Chapter 2). The Bullock Report (1975) was commissioned by the government to address disaffection and underachievement of black pupils. Recommendations included those for a multicultural curriculum to be applied across all phases to provide a more relevant curriculum for black pupils. Curriculum content determined as culturally relevant through policy decisions has been popularly summarised as the 'Three S's of Saris, Samosas and Steel Bands' (Troyna and Carrington, 1990). This phrase encapsulates the characteristics of an uncritical multiculturalism that focuses on ethnic differences and cultural stereotypes, distracting from pervading issues of economic power, whiteness and advantage operating as major discriminating factors in society. The phrase 'tourist-multiculturalism' describes the tokenism of multicultural education in the early years sector through curriculum resources and celebrations of festivals (Derman-Sparks, 1993). Although multiculturalism can be acknowledged as a well-meaning and significant step forward at the time, if not framed by a critical approach to challenge institutional and covert practices it can exclude diversity and promote hierarchies of whiteness. Multiculturalism can then perpetuate inequalities rather than challenge them, becoming part of the hidden curriculum that transmits dominant ideologies. By omission, the inclusive contribution that diverse communities make to education and society are excluded and devalued in education. Consequently, black children may be othered and marginalised within the curriculum and mainstream culture of the school (Scheurich and Young, 1997; Gillborn, 2008; Ladson-Billings, 2009). Such processes are apparent in recruitment of staff, pupil intake, assessment content and methods, disciplinary codes, and peer and adult relationships, as well as curriculum organisation and content. The physical environment may portray images that marginalise black children and teaching resources may exclude and stereotype through cultural irrelevance.

The experiences of the children in this book are underpinned by a non-critical multiculturalism that is common practice in many early years settings. Festivals relevant to the diverse communities are celebrated with corresponding classroom activities, such as St. Patrick's Day cards and the Diwali lamps in Sonic's and Kylie's story (Chapter 4). These celebrations include assemblies and special events but are separate from common curriculum delivery and activity. Black history month is celebrated in all four schools with activities organised by predominantly white practitioners but implemented by black ancillary staff and parents. These include African drumming, cooking national dishes and exhibiting displays of famous black personalities. The annual events can be seen as exoticising children's cultures as the content is not systematically incorporated into the everyday curriculum. Isolated topics are planned through activities such as self-portrait collages and paintings without opportunities to discuss feelings about difference in appearances. Implementation focuses on artistic technique and representation, missing opportunities to raise issues of how racialised identities are perceived by the children. Without this sharing of ideas, the activities may perpetuate stereotypes predetermined through racial hierarchies based on appearance, as indicated in Pina's story (Chapter 5). Exoticising cultures through non-critical multiculturalism can contribute to alienating children from a British identity. This could also be said of an exhibition of children's photos in the main corridor of one school displaying name captions and denoting the origins of families linked to a large map of the world. Corresponding captions state that all children represented on the display are from the country of family origin rather than acknowledging those who are British by birth. In a second school this unintentional othering process is replicated in a classroom display of flags drawn by the children but again labelled by reference to where children come from. The captions might be seen to represent a colour-blind approach by a conception of nationality formed through notions of white Britishness. Dawn's story (Chapter 6) further explores issues around how dominant whiteness prevents critical awareness of the impact of the hidden curriculum on the marginalisation of black children.

Whiteness can be normalised by invisibility in the classroom through the hidden curriculum such as in classroom procedures, curriculum and social norms, including those of behaviour (Robinson and Jones Diaz, 2006, p. 66). Black parents are aware of how the predominance of whiteness excludes others from the environment and curriculum. As a partial response to their marginalisation, children as young as 5 years have been attending black supplementary schools since the late 1970s. These are private and voluntary tutorial schools held out of school hours. Some parents consider them as more culturally and educationally relevant to black children than are white-dominated institutions that can fail their children. Popularity of supplementary education is based on a view that in mainstream education there can be a risk of stereotyping and a lack of understanding of cultural differences or failure to adapt teaching styles to meet black children's educational needs (Majors, 2001). They 'create a space of blackness' where children feel they can challenge the white values of mainstream schooling (Reay and Mirza, 2001, p. 97). It is important to understand how processes at institutional and personal levels disengage black families and undermine their confidence that schools can represent their children's educational needs and provide a relevant learning environment. Critical consciousness in personal perceptions and interpretations of relationships with others can be a first step towards challenging bias (Ang, 2010). This includes an understanding of how whiteness maintains privilege and power in society through everyday interactions. Implicit bias is a current term used to define unconscious racism that can be inherent and invisible (BBC Analysis, 2017). This may be transmitted through a non-critical multiculturalism, contributing to the racialisation of children who are not representative of the predominant school culture.

The detachment or marginalisation of school knowledge from children's lived experiences can be a cause of disaffection towards the formal curriculum. Content is not always relevant to their personal realities and does not give them voice to oppose their racialisation. This is the experience of my 9-year-old black granddaughter performing in a Shakespeare play at her primary school. When practicing her lines, she protests that she 'hates' Shakespeare because it has nothing to do with her life and she does not understand it. She is a keen reader who enjoys books by authors who tell stories to which she can relate using familiar language and images. All children should be exposed to aspects of language and literature inherent in British culture. However, introduction must be in context with their development and cultural understandings, as with all forms of new knowledge. When imposed through curriculum requirements determined centrally, new experiences can become culturally meaningless. Some families are seeking alternative curriculum initiatives to multicultural education, such as an African-centred approach. In addition to providing images of black culture and communities, this pedagogy is inclusive of black history and achievements and is suggested as providing a more relevant and inclusive education for black children (Graham, 2001). It is important to provide a relevant curriculum that includes and initiates discussion about children's experiences outside school, offering opportunities to include them rather than marginalise them through a tokenistic multicultural content.

Curriculum reforms and the inclusion of black pupils

In the late 1980s the Education Reform Act (ERA) (DfE, 1988) introduced the compulsory National Curriculum. The curriculum has been criticised as being 'predominantly Eurocentric, Anglo-centric and mono-cultural and largely unrepresentative of a multi-cultural and multi-racial society' (Verma, 1999, p. 3). Curriculum content restricts the ability of practitioners to adapt teaching to the particular relevance of children as it requires a standardised approach and regular assessment through testing. The ideological shift in early years education policy was one from laissez-faire, before the introduction of the National Curriculum, towards progression of curriculum formality and achievement of prescribed outcomes. Lea (2014) proposes that this approach ensures education of the youngest children serves to reproduce existing raced, gendered and classed privileges.

Official government guidance for the early years education sector began with the introduction of an assessment framework, the Desirable Outcomes for Children's Learning (DfE, 1996). The Department for Education (DfE) has since revised curriculum guidance documents for children aged 0–5 years, with the most recent published in 2017. Recommendations in both the original and revised documents reflect a multicultural ideology of individualism and respect for cultures with few references to the impact of race and racism on young children. The guiding principles of early years care and education include statements recognising that every child should be viewed as unique and experiences should respond to their individual needs. This is through action towards 'equality of opportunity' and 'anti-discriminatory practice', including the need for a strong partnership between parents and practitioners (DfE, 2017a, pp. 5, 6). The curriculum document emphasises that children must know about 'similarities and differences' in 'families, communities and traditions' (DfE, 2017a, p. 12). Outside a critical reflective pedagogy, this requirement in the specific area of Understanding the World can be interpreted from a tokenistic multicultural perspective through celebrations of festivals outside the general curriculum. In the assessment document accompanying the English Curriculum Guidance, the Early Learning Goal states that children must not only understand difference and similarity but that diversity must be treated with respect. A respect for difference can become tokenistic unless children have opportunities to discuss feelings and ideas they have internalised about diversity. This approach questions children's negative ideas of difference and attitudes to racialised hierarchies. The Early Years Profile Handbook gives opportunities for interpretation through a critical pedagogy in the section entitled Children from Minority Groups (DfE, 2017b, pp. 19–20). To promote attainment children should be 'enabled to represent their positive cultural experiences within the learning environment'. The statement indicates the importance of building on home experiences and 'things which are familiar to them' to support learning. There is a later reference to practitioners understanding and listening to children expressing their feelings in relation to 'the environment and social situations' to facilitate confidence in learning. These principles go some way towards support-ing the particular needs of children from diverse cultural backgrounds, although issues of racialisation are not signified as important elements in children's learner identities.

The racialisation of children has a negative impact on all children's social rela-tionships, impacting on learning dispositions (Bradbury, 2013). It is important to raise issues of stereotyping and racial hierarchies with children as they arise, affording opportunities to discuss attitudes and consequences from both personal and societal perspectives. The curriculum guidance does not advise or include examples of how practitioners can raise issues with children. During a recent visit to a reception classroom, I observed children discussing stereotypes they had formed about people from different religions. The practitioner led the discussion from the perspective of a current news item as an approach to depersonalise their views. This enabled the children to speak freely about how they formed personal perceptions and enabled challenges to stereotypes. Discussions with children in early years settings can be initiated when discriminatory practices are observed in everyday interactions to contextualise more abstract concepts. By demonstrating awareness of racialising experiences, children will feel more able to raise issues as they occur. Onye, a 4-year-old child with African heritage in my nursery, was fre-quently called by the name 'onion' by children. He was also observed washing his hands frequently. When asked why, he replied 'to wash the black off'. The boy was so distressed by the daily micro-aggressions he experienced that his mother asked if we could call him Peter rather than Onye. Nursery policy was to call children by their given name to reflect their heritage despite many requests by parents to use a common English name. The requests were in response to mispronunciation, misspelling and derogatory abbreviation that commonly occurred in society. It was agreed that we should celebrate his name in context with the names of other children and their families along with implications on identities. A project was planned to celebrate names while promoting understanding of the implications of racialised attitudes and name-calling on social and emotional development. The reasons for the project were discussed between practitioners and parents and a wall chart was completed with all children that depicted their names and what it meant for them. Discussions took place with children individually as the chart was made, followed up in small and large groups. Correct pronunciation of children's names acknowledged their identities and became the norm for children. Resources, books and incidents during everyday activity supported further sessions related to the effects of racial micro-aggressions. Discussions were in context with children's experiences and attitudes as they emerged during interactions. These actions raised issues not only of how children experience racism but also of how white children can treat others unjustly through unquestioned acceptance of their cultural norms. Although the insults towards Onye's name would probably have a lasting effect, the project was aimed at supporting him and other children to challenge racism and maintain positive identities in the face of future racialising experiences. A postscript to this incident occurred 2 years later when Onye's mother was admitted to hospital with mental health problems that her husband assigned to issues of racism in the community where they lived. A recommendation in the EYFS Profile Handbook (DfE, 2017b) to communicate with parents to better understand social situations implies an understanding of how discrimination in society impacts on children's development. Dawn's story (Chapter 6) illustrates how, without support through both publications and training, it is difficult to understand the invisibility of whiteness and the covert racialisation processes in society that impact on black children's education and psychological well-being. By centring race in black children's lives through a critical theoretical framework such as CRT, the hidden curriculum and racialising experiences can be addressed at micro and macro levels in early years education.

Action towards critical multicultural education

The anti-racist movement in education emerged to address the ineffectiveness of multicultural education and to challenge systemic racism in institutional procedures in schools. A more direct and formal recognition of racism in British schools and its links with the underachievement of black pupils came initially through the White Paper *Excellence in Schools* (DfE, 1997). This was initiated mainly as a response from the newly elected Labour government to the colour-blind approach in previous education policy discourse and legislation. A report (MacPherson, 1988) published in response to the murder of a black teenager Stephen Lawrence added an emphasis on racism at institutional level. The acknowledgement of institutional racism resulted in legislation through the Race Relations Amendment Act, 2000 (RRA Act), making it unlawful for institutions in England to discriminate on the grounds of race and ethnicity. This included a requirement for internal policies to challenge racism. The Commission for Racial Equality (CRE) published standards for racial equality in schools in *Learning for All* (CRE, 2000), focusing on achievement and good practice to promote racial equality. A section on attitudes and environment gives guidance with a strong message to monitor and act on incidents of racism. This reflects a policy shift away from non-critical multiculturalism to one of direct anti-racist action to challenge and prevent structural as well as personal racism. Following publication of the standards, racial discrimination is officially recognised at all levels in education. Legislation resulted in an activist anti-racist approach adopted successfully within some individual institutions, although little change is evident at a macro level with black pupils still underachieving today. This is partly a consequence of a lack of strategic commitment to address institutional racism in schools and consistent government-led monitoring of anti-racist practice not being seen as a priority during inspections (Gillborn, 2016).

CRT is emerging in England as an alternative anti-racist framework to centre racism in action towards social justice (Chapter 1). CRT precepts provide a theoretical frame through which to openly address race and racism in both institutional and personal interactions. A direct approach that accepts the existence of racism as disadvantaging othered communities can support effective early years practice. Chapter 8 suggests how this can be achieved by establishing a culture that recognises racism as an inherent historical legacy, perpetuated through institutional and structural processes, potentially exacerbated by implicit and unconscious bias. The children's stories in this book give insight into how, by listening to their voices and interpreting their experiences through a CRT lens, action can be taken towards a more inclusive learning environment.

Partnerships between black parents and early years settings

The importance of home-school partnerships to support children's learning has been a priority in early years education since the early Plowden Report included a section promoting the notion of 'parents as partners' (CACE, 1967). The EPPE (2004) research project has also highlighted the contribution that parents make to their children's early education. The study indicates that effective settings develop good communication strategies for practitioners and parents to share information and decision-making regarding children's learning. Despite this tradition in early years policy, practitioners can still have difficulties engaging with parents. Regular contact with parents is not always seen as necessary, with communication taking too much time away from internal and external demands for accountability. The needs of parents can be seen to replace valuable opportunities for interaction with children within an already over-demanding schedule. Another concern may be that involvement of parents is a threat to teachers' autonomy, as parents could interfere with decisions without knowledge of confidential internal factors (Vincent, 1996). These concerns partly result from an overburden of bureaucratic reporting, preventing essential dialogue that challenges implicit bias and provides insight to children's external experiences that may impact on their learning. Although Vincent's research was more than two decades ago, the current managerial culture still results in similar barriers to communication.

An additional influence on participation arises from a hierarchical status between staff and parents (Dixson and Rousseau, 2006). This is exacerbated by the marginalisation of children's cultures and languages. Parents may feel unwelcome or not valued for their contribution. Vincent found that these unequal power relationships between parents and teachers resulted in 'black groups and individuals often responding with disillusionment and suspicion of the white-dominated education system' (1996, p. 76). Bad experiences during their own education may also impact on black parents' views of school. The institutional environment can remind them of conflict with teachers and low expectations alongside exclusion from their own school days (Rollock et al., 2015). It may then be difficult to relate to white middle-class values in their children's schools, inducing feelings of disempowerment and reluctance to participate. More meaningful partnerships can be developed through an understanding of the effects of race and racism on professional and personal interactions, overcoming racialised barriers.

Some schemes aimed at encouraging parents to participate can be tokenistic and viewed as patronising. Parents may also feel ineffective as educators of their children if their contribution is not valued and seen as peripheral, such as only in annual festival celebrations. A divide can widen through requests for participation if not substantial or in context with everyday curriculum activity, causing parents to opt out of involvement throughout their child's education. In their study on parental engagement in early years services, Page, Whitting and Mclean (2007) found that the lack of participation was due to a colour-blind approach to the particular social and cultural circumstances of parents. Lack of knowledge of home circumstances created a barrier to participation during both the day and evening. Demands on parents were not considered when organising events or opportunities for supporting children. This can result in non-engagement in traditional forms of interaction such as completing homework records or attending termly progress meetings (Chapman, 2006). Although these are an important part of school routines, parents may view such initiatives as tokenistic outside more regular and meaningful communication. An indication of how misunderstandings can occur is an account of how a white middle-class teacher's perceptions and expectations of a 'good parent' reading a story at bedtime conflicts with some working class black parents' ability to participate in the school initiative (Zamudio et al., 2011, pp. 137–140). Social factors such as working hours, childcare, transportation, and translation services, alongside culturally specific routines, can prevent the bedtime story, which is a cultural tradition for the white teacher. It can be assumed that the parents are not interested in their children's education because of their lack of participation in the school project without an understanding of any impinging social factors. Parents are often judged through unfair assumptions formed through stereotypes of their cultural backgrounds (Bradbury, 2013). Research projects including those of Mirza (2009), Sewell (2010) and Rollock et al. (2015) have found that black parents make their children's education of central importance by supporting them at home and when possible through expenditure on resources and tuition. By listening to perspectives of parents and discussing diverse views and experiences, hierarchical power relations can be dissipated. Meaningful and trusting partnerships can then be formed between practitioners and parents.

Summary

This chapter has discussed how black children's education can be enriched in an environment where practitioners offer appropriate opportunities for them to develop a value-free identity that positively includes their blackness and cultural wealth. An early years pedagogy centred in the ideology of play and self-directed activity must be framed by a critical awareness of how race and racism impact on black children's first contacts with an early years setting and their everyday interactions in the environment. The precepts of CRT discussed in this book can support a critical early years pedagogy that recognises processes such as racial micro-aggressions and colour-blindness, through which black children are stereotyped and excluded across racialised, classed and gendered identities. Action can then be taken to address these processes at both personal and institutional levels to challenge the hierarchical values placed on whiteness that impact on learner identities. Substantive systems can be put in place to communicate with parents to understand their perceptions of the early years environment and to involve and inform them of their children's learning through a playful pedagogy. Chapter 8 contributes to this process with suggestions for both individual and whole team action towards a reflective pedagogy that supports children from minority groups, as required in the DfE early years guidance documents.

Reflective practice

- Do you have opportunities to discuss how children learn through play with their parents? What evidence can you share with parents to reassure them that developmental targets are met during child-initiated activity?
- Multicultural education has been discussed in this chapter as possibly exclusive rather than inclusive. How can you ensure inclusivity throughout the early years curriculum to avoid the predominance of whiteness and the marginalisation of some children?

References

Ang, L. (2010) Critical Perspectives on Cultural Diversity in Early Childhood: Building an Inclusive Curriculum and Provision, in *Early Years*, 30 (1) pp. 41–52.

BBC Analysis (2017) *Implicit Bias*. Available from BBC iPlayer. Accessed 20 June 2017.

Bradbury, A. (2013) *Understanding Early Years Inequality: Policy, Assessment and Young Children's Identities*. Oxon: Routledge.

Broadhead, P. and Burt, A. (2012) *Understanding Young Children's Learning through Play*. Oxon: Routledge.

Brooker, L. (2010) Learning to Play in a Cultural Context, in Broadhead, P., Howard, J. and Wood, E. (eds.), *Play and Learning in the Early Years*. London: Sage Publications.

Bullock, A. (1975) *A Language for Life*. London: Her Majesty's Stationary Office.

Cambridge Primary Review (2009) Towards a New Primary Curriculum, in *Cambridge Primary Review*. Cambridge: Cambridge University Faculty of Education.

Campbell, S. (2005) Secret Children's Business, in Yelland, N. (ed.), *Critical Issues in Early Childhood Education*. Berkshire: Open University Press.

Central Advisory Council for England (CACE) (1967) *Children and Their Primary Schools: Plowden Report.* London: Her Majesty's Stationary Office.

Chapman, T. K. (2006) Pedaling Backwards, in Dixson, A. and Rousseau, D. (eds.), *Critical Race Theory in Education.* Oxon: Routledge.

Commission for Racial Equality (CRE) (2000) *Learning for All, Standards for Racial Equality in Schools.* London: Belmont Press.

Department for Education (DfE) (1988) *Education Reform Act.* Available from www.legislation. gov.uk.

Department for Education (DfE) (1996) *Nursery Education: Desirable Outcomes for Children's Learning on Entering Compulsory Education.* London: School Standards Curriculum Authority (SSCA).

DfE (2017a) *Statutory Framework for the Early Years Foundation Stage: Setting the Standards for Learning, Development and Care for Children from Birth to Five.* London: Her Majesty's Stationary Office.

DfE (2017b) *Early Years Foundation Stage Profile Handbook.* London: Her Majesty's Stationary Office.

Derman-Sparks, L. (1993) Revisiting Multicultural Education: What Children Need to Live in a Diverse Society, in *Dimensions of Early Childhood*, 22 (1) pp. 6–10.

Dixson, A. and Rousseau, C. (2006) The First Day of School: A CRT Story, in Dixson, A. and Rousseau, C. (eds.), *Critical Race Theory in Education.* Oxon: Routledge.

Effective Provision of Pre-School Education (EPPE) (2004) *Effective Provision of Pre-School Education Project: Final Report.* Available from www.surestart.gov.uk.

Gillborn, D. (2008) *Racism and Education, Coincidence or Conspiracy.* Oxon: Routledge.

Gillborn, D. (2016) White Lies: Things That Were Told about Race and Education That Weren't True. Available from www.birmingham.ac.uk/schools/education/research/2016/ gillborn. Accessed 5 December 2016.

Giroux, H. A. (1997) *Pedagogy and the Politics of Hope.* Colorado, USA: Westview Press.

Giroux, H. A. (2009) Teacher Education and Democratic Schooling, in Darder, A., Baltodano, M. and Torres, R. (eds.), *The Critical Pedagogy Reader.* Oxon: Routledge.

Graham, M. (2001) Toward an African-Centred Orientation towards Knowledge, in Majors, R. (ed.), *Educating Our Black Children: New Directions and Radical Approaches.* Oxon: Routledge.

Guishard-Pine, J. (2010) *Psychology, Race Equality and Working with Children.* Staffordshire: Trentham Books.

Lea, S. (2014) Early Years Work, Professionalism and the Translation of Policy into Practice, in Kingdon, Z. and Gourd, J. (eds.), *Early Years Policy: The Impact on Practice.* Oxon: Routledge.

Ladson-Billings, G. (2009) Just What Is CRT and What's It Doing in a Nice Field Like Education, in Taylor, E., Gillborn, D. and Ladson-Billings, G. (eds.), *Foundations of Critical Race Theory in Education.* Oxon: Routledge.

MacGregor-Smith, R. (2017) *Race in the Workplace, the MacGregor-Smith Review.* Available from www.gov.uk>publications>race-in-the-workplace. Accessed 10 December 2017.

MacNaughton, G. (2003) *Shaping Early Childhood.* Berkshire: Open University Press.

MacPherson, W. (1999) *The Stephen Lawrence Inquiry.* London: HMSO.

Majors, R. (2001) Introduction, in Majors, R. (ed.), *Educating Our Black Children: New Directions and Radical Approaches.* London: Routledge Falmer.

McDowall Clark, R. (2017) *Exploring the Contexts for Early Learning: Challenging the School Readiness Agenda.* Oxon: Routledge.

Mirza, H. S. (2009) *Race, Gender and Educational Desire: Why Black Women Succeed and Fail.* Oxon: Routledge.

Page, J., Whitting, Dr. G. and Mclean, C. (2007) *Engaging Affectively with Black and Minority Ethnic Parents in Children's and Parental Services.* Available from www.dcfs.gov.uk/ research. Accessed 25 January 2015.

Reay, D. and Mirza, H. (2001) Black Supplementary Schools, in Majors, R. (ed.), *Educating Our Black Children: New Directions and Radical Approaches*. London: Routledge Falmer.

Robinson, K. and Jones Diaz, C. (2006) *Diversity and Difference in Early Childhood Education*. Berkshire: Open University Press.

Rogoff, B. (2003) *The Cultural Nature of Human Development*. Oxford: Open University Press.

Rollock, N., et al. (2015) *The Colour of Class*. Oxon: Routledge.

Scheurich, J. and Young, M. (1977) Coloring Epistemologies: Are Our Research Epistemologies Racially Biased? in *Educational Research*, 26 (4) pp. 4–16. New York: Sage Publications.

Sewell, T. (1996) *Black Masculinities and Schooling: How Black Boys Survive Modern Schooling*. Staffordshire: Trentham Books.

Sewell, T. (2010) Overcoming the 'Triple Quandary': How Black Students Navigate the Obstacles of Achievement, in Ochieng, B. M. N. and Hylton, C. L. A. (eds.), *Black Families in Britain as the Site of Struggle*. Manchester: Manchester University Press.

Sillin, J. (2005) Silence Voice and Pedagogy, in Yelland, N. (ed.), *Critical Issues in Early Childhood Education*. Berkshire: Open University Press.

Thompson, L. (2014) Keynote Lecture: True and False Self and Proxy Identities in Black and Minority Ethnic Children, in *Proceedings of the Seminar Thinking Spaces, July 3 2014, London*. Tavistock and Portman NHS Foundation Trust. Swiss Cottage, London.

Troyna, B. and Carrington, B. (1990) *Education, Racism and Reform*. London: Routledge.

Van Ausdale, D. and Feagin, J. R. (2001) *The First R.: How Children Learn Race and Racism*. Lanham, Maryland USA: Rowman and Littlefield.

Verma, G. (1999) Cultural and Religious Diversity within the National Curriculum, in Drury, B. (ed.), *Education, the Education Reform Act (1988) and Racial Equality, in Ethnic Relations No. 7*. Coventry: Warwick University.

Vincent, C. (1996) *Parent and Teachers, Power and Participation*. London: Falmer Press.

Vygotsky, L. (1986) *Thought and Language*. Cambridge, MA, USA: The MIT Press.

Wood, E. (2010) Developing Integrated Pedagogical Approaches to Play and Learning, in Broadhead, P., Howard, J. and Wood, E. (eds.), *Play and Learning in the Early Years*. London: Sage Publications.

Zamudio, M., Russell, C., Rios, F. and Bridgeman, J. (eds.) (2011) *Critical Race Theory Matters: Education and Ideology*. Oxon: Routledge.

8

THE WAY FORWARD

Action towards a more inclusive early years education

Introduction

The stories in this book emphasise that action is an essential element of the early years agenda to support black children in what is often their first independent experience outside the home and as a foundation for their future education. This chapter introduces ways in which practice can be reviewed towards providing an environment that substantially addresses inequalities. There is an emphasis throughout this book for the need to hear the voices of all children in early years settings regarding attitudes to race. Children's stories give an insight into the impact of racism on social relationships, identities and early education. To understand the cultural nuances within settings that contribute to processes of racialisation, there needs to be an awareness of how interactions within the white spaces of the environment impact on their daily experiences (Rollock et al., 2015). The children's stories in this book indicate the importance of supporting black children to challenge their racialisation by addressing the factors that reproduce racism in early years education. In these times when there are so many requirements for accountability through formal assessments and observations it is difficult to find time to stand back and listen to what children can tell us about themselves. A business model of leadership and administrative demands can obstruct opportunities to observe how taken for granted procedures may unintentionally marginalise black children. The recommendations below introduce ways in which these issues can be reviewed within everyday procedures and practices so as to provide an environment that substantially addresses inequalities. The activities suggested are for all practitioners regardless of their personal or professional identities. Dawn's story (Chapter 6) illustrates how discussion between colleagues with diverse views and perspectives can provide invaluable insights into how racism is reproduced and how it impacts differently to either advantage or disadvantage lives. Open, honest debate within a no-blame culture enables practitioners to work together when addressing issues that counteract the general aim of providing equality for all.

It is important to raise awareness in teams of more covert aspects of racism discussed throughout this book. Establishment of a no-blame culture in the setting can alleviate inhibitions regarding discussion of personal attitudes and ideas about race by placing them in a historically grounded social context that inevitably impacts on everyone (Lane, 2008). Some may choose to begin by discussion and analysis of the stories in this book to address situations in their own settings or that may have personal relevance. Others may prefer to start with pertinent issues arising in the setting. Establishing an anti-racist ethos cannot be achieved overnight, as it will depend on different levels of experience and understanding. Action should occur at a pace relevant to each setting and each practitioner's experiences. An approach to raising issues and gaining consensus for action should be a decision that takes account of both personal perspectives and professional priorities. The suggestions in this chapter are for both teams and individuals to recognise how black children are racialised through everyday activity. The process for change can then be determined both personally and jointly with colleagues. Although small steps can be taken, an environment that systematically acts against racism at all levels may take some time. Without understanding and acknowledgement of the diverse ways in which children are racialised, change may be superficial and simply reflect a non-critical multiculturalism that further marginalises black children (Chapter 7). The stories in this book emphasise that action is an essential element of the early years agenda to support black children in what is often their first independent experience outside the home. The suggestions below can be a start to ongoing action or they may trigger other ideas that relate closer to the individual circumstances in settings and personal journeys towards providing a strong foundation for black children's future education.

Establishing a no-blame culture

This book provides research evidence that young children are as aware of race and racist attitudes as they are of other aspects of discrimination such as gender and disability. Stereotypes have been discussed as being formed through the media alongside personal interactions in homes and communities. To enable children to voice their understanding of diversity, time should be made available for practitioners to observe how attitudes are reproduced in the setting and how black children are using their agency to challenge racialisation. For this it is important to create an ethos in which the team can feel able to discuss ideas about race and so gain insight into the implications for policies, procedures and attitudes. As Dawn's story shows, our personal and social histories impact on who we are and how we think about society. Socially derived concepts of othered communities give rise to preformed attitudes and stereotypes about those who differ from ourselves. Practitioners have a professional responsibility to address discrimination as it disadvantages all children when not challenged. A topic could be raised either in the whole team or between individual colleagues through an observation or example of a child's behaviour. This can be the starting point to depersonalise discussions that may initially be difficult to talk about in a team. A black child in my nursery who spent much time in the creative art area refused to use any colour but pink when drawing or painting her own face. This was discussed in a team meeting and the multiracial team offered many different perspectives on why this might be. Discussions continued informally after the meeting as practitioners began to consider how their own attitudes formed their reasoning regarding why the child chose pink. Following the open debate arising from just one observation, practitioners felt more able to raise a range of personal views and stereotypes regarding cultures and racialised identities. Practitioners became more aware of how personal attitudes towards race and gender impacted on the children as well as on their own professional and social lives. They were able to raise issues and understand how negative stereotypes are formed and can be challenged through the reality of experiences. The initial observation opened up ongoing debate and action regarding other incidents in the setting. Practitioners' perspectives on the intersections of identity can be challenged and rethought through this process and action determined against processes and attitudes that create barriers against social and educational opportunities.

Personal reflections – towards equality

It is important to reflect on personal histories to understand the acquisition of racialised concepts as the norm and how, when and where stereotypes are acquired about particular communities. Childhood experiences of books and resources bought for them in the home are powerful influences in the forma-tion of stereotypes. Popular stories of Enid Blyton's Famous Five and the reading scheme Janet and John gave my generation and those following false ideas of a desirable society based on whiteness and middle-class values. This was alongside toys that stereotyped black people. Resources can now be purchased that are more representational of British society through companies such as Letterbox Library and on the internet. However, toys such as good-quality black dolls remain rare in high-street shops and when available are more expensive. It is easier and cheaper to buy dolls with European facial features that are brown instead of pink. Although children from diverse cultures and racialised identities are represented more often in books for children, there still remains a predominance of images and texts representing white middle-class values. Practitioners could be given the opportunity to discuss their own childhood experiences of toys and books that either supported attitudes to themselves and others or have influenced negative stereotypes. This can be through informal sessions in which small groups are given a list of factors to consider when selecting resources relevant to children in their setting. I remember when I selected some costly books for my nursery in the Jolly Postman series because I thought they were innovative in their presen-tation and would appeal to young children. Children ignored the books despite efforts of practitioners to gain their interest. In the books the postman delivered post to isolated houses within the greenery of the countryside where there was an all-white community engaged in activities unfamiliar to the children. Communication was through letters rather than more current methods of phone or internet. The stories and images did not appeal to the children, as they did not relate to their urban lives or their racialised identities. By choosing these books, my own whiteness and middle-class culture unintentionally excluded most of the children in the setting through irrelevance. By rejecting the books they were actively expressing the marginalisation of their home cultures and the concept of whiteness as Britishness. The staff team was conscious of the children's voices when selecting future resources by including a checklist for recognising bias. Either examples or personal experiences could be an introduction to a team session aimed at raising how attitudes can be so culturally and historically ingrained that they can remain invisible.

Alternatively, each person could give an example in writing of how their stereotypes have been formed either as a child or as an adult. If members of the team are not ready to give personal examples, pro formas could be completed that include common stereotypes in British society such as those raised in this book:

- Black children are good at sports and music.
- Black parents are not interested in their children's education.
- Black children are often late to school.

Written ideas can be shared in meetings either anonymously or by the individuals concerned. Through personal reflection or in whole teams, practitioners could consider how these ideas may have arisen and how they have influenced their own attitudes and ways of thinking. Discussion either in teams or one-to-one with colleagues can encourage practitioners to reflect on their own biases and experiences of racism. This is not to place blame but to bring about a realisation of how stereotypes are acquired. An analysis of experiences makes it possible to question and confront attitudes through reflection regarding the consequences on oneself and others, facilitating action for both personal and professional change.

The timescale necessary for this process would vary for practitioners, whether alone, through group activity or during informal discussions. Those practitioners who experience racism might not feel able to share with colleagues who may not understand the impact or may question their interpretations. Those for whom the reality of racism is not part of their lives may need longer to realise the ways in which racism is conveyed through personal attitudes, interactions and institutional practices. Awareness of the effects of racism can be better understood through acknowledgement of how life experiences inevitably form attitudes including unconscious bias that must be challenged. The appropriate pace towards action for change will depend on each individual. Creating an environment in which it is safe for all to share can be achieved through depersonalisation of the processes that result in racism. Racism has been embedded in British society during eras of slavery, colonisation and subsequent changes in society through historic and current immigration. It has resurfaced in the media recently through Brexit and the immigration debate, as discussed in the early chapters of this book. By reviewing personal attitudes in context with historical facts, it becomes easier to consider influences on racialising experiences and take responsibility for addressing personal attitudes. New understandings should go alongside recognition of social and personal responsibility for change that can provide supportive and relevant early years environment for young black children.

Practical action to support a critical anti-racist pedagogy

Once practitioners feel secure to discuss their own attitudes and understand the effects of racism on young children, regular discussions can take place more easily during everyday activity. This gives opportunities for ongoing awareness and development of ideas through personal and strategic review of the hidden curriculum. Aspects of the hidden curriculum that influence racialisation have been highlighted throughout this book and include the following:

- The ethos of the setting, including environmental resources such as displays and notices
- Curriculum content and resources
- Curriculum delivery and organisation
- Children's relationships and interactions during play and other activity
- Assessment content and methods
- Opportunities for communication with parents
- Enrolment and settling-in procedures
- Recruitment and retention of staff
- Roles and responsibilities within the staff team

The team could also challenge bias through reviews of policy and procedures using guidance such as the following:

- How the needs of black children are viewed in the setting
- How play and learning resources are selected and provided
- How daily routines provide for diverse cultural norms
- How languages are supported

These are suggestions under broad categories, and decisions can be made regarding setting priorities at micro and macro levels in consideration of issues that are impacting on equality. Changes should be monitored to maintain consistency of action as other priorities can make demands on time. By opening up discussions about attitudes and how they can be understood outside personal blame and guilt, stereotypes can be dismissed as false and practitioners can revise approaches towards action for equality and social justice.

Listening to young children to understand their experiences of racialisation

As well as discussion with colleagues, it is important to listen to the voices of the children from othered communities to understand their racialising experiences and attitudes as those in this book have indicated. This section considers how practitioners can provide time in their busy schedules to observe how children are racialised through procedures and practices of the setting. Chapter 1 explained how CRT enables a focus on hearing the views of othered communities in society by prioritising their voices to understand experiences of racialisation. Observations of children are an integral aspect of early years practice to support children's development and to reveal the personal, unique needs of each child. Analysis underpinned by acknowledgement of race and racism can give greater insight into the processes by which settings may marginalise and racialise black children. Children are frequently not listened to from their personal perspectives as the current management culture demands accountability through externally monitored milestones. Observations guided by developmental targets leave few opportunities for interpretation from children's personal priorities. The children's stories emphasise the need to observe the influence of racialised interactions on children's experiences and how they challenge marginalisation and stereotyping. Awareness of the processes that may exclude black children can frame action towards change at all levels in early years education.

Although race equality has taken a low priority in recent government initiatives, the reduction in official monitoring should not result in early years settings abandoning previous initiatives aimed at challenging racism. It is important to support children during their early experiences through naturalistic observations that identify influences on their identities and cultural nuances. The stories told in this book indicate that racialisation cannot be understood through single incidents but must be interpreted through ongoing, sometimes seemingly insignificant, experiences such as the hair pulling in Pina's story. It is possible to do this through already established observation routines by including an additional category for the intersections of equality issues, including aspects such as the following:

- Are British identities reflected in resources?
- Are children using home languages and dialects and when? How do practitioners and peers react?
- Are children representing cultural knowledge and wealth during play, and if so what makes this possible?
- Are children excluded/included during play and are cultural hierarchies used to manipulate others?

The key worker system is invaluable for supporting equality by using strategies to address issues for particular children. Team schedules could include times for substantive key worker discussions with parents using narrative records of activity alongside existing sessions to share more formal records of development. Vignettes written in the setting and by the family at home can give snapshots of children's experiences. Sharing them can provide a more holistic understanding of support that can be given for the child in the setting and at home. Discussions with parents can reveal socio-cultural aspects of home life, countering stereotypes that might impact on interpretation of observations as in Kylie's experiences (Chapter 4). Additional perspectives make it possible to stand back from whiteness to analyse observations from a position of the black child. MacNaughton et al. (2007) propose three questions to inform racialised power relations in the classroom to challenge whiteness in interpretation and understanding of observations:

- What power relations have already been accomplished and how do these touch children and their understandings about themselves and others?
- Where are the dangers and possibilities for racially just and equitable relationships and understandings with children?
- How is racialised power circulating through us and our practices and desires and what effects is it having on the possibility for social justice in our early childhood communities?

(2007, p. 176)

As well as being a useful guide to countering any preformed ideas when interpreting children's activity, these questions can support challenges to the hierarchy of whiteness within both personal and institutional practices.

Understanding how whiteness contributes to the marginalisation of others

CRT is suggested (Chapter 1) as a way of understanding how black children can be excluded in the white middle-class environment dominant in many education institutions (Leonardo, 2009). Whiteness is not about appearance, although this is a visible, physical contributory factor in the racialisation of young children. Whiteness is viewed in CRT as a social construct to maintain status quo and power in society (Chapter 1). It is about how aspects of society are accepted as unquestionable norms without analysis of the effects on those who can be disadvantaged and marginalised in a racialised hierarchy. Whiteness and its relationship to power are located within everyday experiences through children's relationships with peers and practitioners, through the environment and through setting procedures. A conceptualisation of whiteness helps identify how such ideas contribute to the racialisation of black children. The English education system beginning in the EYFS and onwards is established through a majority white hierarchical structure from government to a predominantly white management structure in institutions. Outcomes are monitored in each setting by the external inspection processes, which are also influenced through whiteness in government decisions. The EYFS curriculum is established centrally from a Eurocentric approach that can marginalise diversity and be culturally exclusive. This is particularly evident in the teaching of phonics in the literacy element of the curriculum (Chapter 7). If not implemented through a critical awareness of diversity, the early years curriculum can contribute to an accepted cultural hierarchy. By viewing practices in education through a CRT lens that centres race and racism, it is possible to understand how the cultural wealth of others can be excluded and how the intersections of children's identities are marginalised. CRT calls for understanding of the social construction of whiteness as crucial to the education of black children, as it acts to discriminate through everyday interactions while maintaining benefits for some in society.

Dawn's story (Chapter 6) shows how easy it is to take inherent perspectives for granted rather than consider the impact on those who are not from the same cultural backgrounds. In the 1970s, as a young newly appointed head teacher, I was made aware of the influence of whiteness on my decision-making when I spent a large amount of the budget on sand play for both the inside and outside spaces. Children freely made use of these resources, but many of the black children stayed away. Parents gave one reason for this as the difficulty in getting sand out of their hair at home. It is common practice now to provide hair cover for all children in sand play, but this was not something I had considered then from my own white perspective, where it was not a problem. This resulted in the school budget and resources disadvantaging black children while others benefited. I am also aware of the privileges of whiteness when choosing birthday cards for my own black children and grandchildren. Every year I search the shops unsuccessfully for a card with an image of a black child amongst the many depicting white children. This situation is reminiscent of McIntosh's fifty privileges of whiteness (Chapter 1). Children can feel excluded when they receive birthday cards that do not reflect their identities or use sticking plasters labelled as 'flesh pink', as they cannot purchase those that more closely resemble their skin colour. A colleague refused a pink stocking to cover the skeletal of her young son's prosthetic leg. She wrote to the company on more than one occasion to complain and was eventually sent a black stocking that she also refused. Six months and many emails later she eventually received a stocking that more closely represented her son's complexion. These everyday experiences can be understood as insignificant. However, they cause additional stress on black families by contributing to the many racial microaggressions that reinforce the hierarchy of whiteness and racialise children from an early age.

After discussing the above examples as a starting point, white practitioners could devise their personal lists of privileges to promote self-awareness. This activity can be useful as a foundation for reviewing provision in the setting to prevent marginalisation in the curriculum and through organisational processes. It can also be the beginning of stepping outside whiteness and challenging colour-blindness for a more inclusive and equitable early years environment. The experiences of children in this book are examples of how it is essential to begin this process to support them in the challenges to their racialisation.

The children's stories

The children's stories highlight particular aspects of the racialisation of black children as they begin reception class. Discussion and analysis of the stories can be tools for practitioners to reflect on ways to challenge both overt and covert racialising experiences in settings. At the end of each chapter suggestions are made and questions asked to reflect on the issues raised. Contributions from readers' own experiences can enable personal reflection on attitudes to race and experiences of racism. Below are some additional questions to raise individual awareness and review the hidden curriculum:

• What do you know about inventors and heroes from other racialised identities to your own? How can you extend your knowledge and promote this in your setting?
• How many children's books in your setting are by authors who are not white and who reflect the identity of the children in multiracial/cultural Britain? What are the implications of your findings for the children in your setting and how can you address these?
• What do you know about the cultures of the children in your setting and in the wider community? How can you find out more and include them in the broad curriculum rather than only through cultural and religious celebrations?
• Reflect on your own ideas regarding racialised and cultural groups in British society. How did you form these attitudes? What is the evidence for your ideas?
• How can you explore children's ideas of race and identity? Give opportunities for discussion with children and consider how personal identities impact on their reflections.

When addressing individual incidents of racism such as those in Pina's story, it is important to support the child who has been racially abused by recognising the psychological impact and allowing time for discussion with the child and parents. It is equally important to provide ongoing support for the perpetrator to consider the effects of their actions and attitudes on themselves and others. Sessions with groups of children can begin from anonymised incidents observed in the setting or through the use of resources such as books or Persona Dolls (Brown, 2008) that introduce experiences to which children can relate. Critically questioning pre-formed ideas about racialised hierarchies and stereotypes can facilitate understandings of the impact on their own lives and on their interactions with others. This is particularly important in settings with predominantly white staff and children, who have little contact with those from othered communities. When I was teaching in an urban further education college, a group of white students from a rural county visited to 'experience a multicultural environment'. Their tutor was aware that they had no understanding of perspectives other than that of whiteness despite living in multiracial England. The image of their astonishment and silence when in the college cafeteria, and their comments later about the impact on them of so many black students, made me realise how important it is to implement a critical anti-racist pedagogy and environment for all settings regardless of the communities where they are based. Despite the intention of their tutor, one visit to a college cannot change deeply rooted attitudes to difference as they returned to the privileged whiteness of their environment. If discussed with these young adults from the start of their education, the stereotypes and attitudes they formed of people who differed from them could have been challenged. They would then be able to better function as citizens in a multiracial Britain. A white relative of mine is conscious that her 3-year-old son has little contact with black children in their small rural town as there are only white children and practitioners in his nursery. Despite difficulty, she buys him toys and books for home that represent the cultural diversity in Britain, also recommending them to the setting. The resources support her to speak to her son about any negative stereotypes and attitudes he may internalise from the media and his social interactions. These examples can be discussed between practitioners who work in settings where there are a majority of white children to understand the implications for their practice. Action can then be taken to address children's attitudes that may view whiteness as the unspoken hierarchal norm and difference as negative.

Keeping race equality policy alive and meaningful

The Race Relations Act (2000) required schools to have specific race equality policies to challenge racism at both personal and institutional levels in addition to more general equalities policies already in place. Since revised legislation in the Equalities Act (2006), Ofsted inspectors now prioritise aspects of a broader inclusive equalities agenda that has marginalised the focus on race equality. Race is now subsumed under the general equality duties and incorporated into new definitions of equal opportunities (Chapter 7). The focus is on discrimination in society, omitting specific reference to race equality, and this can deflect from more direct approaches that challenge racism at all levels in institutions. The necessity for effective race equality practice should not be dismissed because there is currently a low profile for monitoring. Race equality policy, like all policies, should be regularly reviewed in relation to the consequences for children's education.

Policy formulation, practice and monitoring must include the whole staff team to reach a consensus on meanings and action. It is about recognising the processes within the setting that operate to discriminate and exclude rather than placing responsibility on individual children for disaffection and underachievement. An understanding of structural and institutional factors is central to action against inequalities. Race equality policies often focus on procedures to address racist incidents, but this can be tokenistic if underlying issues that impact on black children's education are not included. Some of these have been highlighted by the children's experiences throughout this book, and factors to consider include the following:

- Consensus regarding the meaning of a racist incident and effective procedures that support those abused and provide action to address the attitudes of perpetrators.
- Ensuring that not only the environment and resources, but also curriculum content, is reflective of many cultures within society generally and relevant to children in the setting.
- Curriculum delivery is appropriate for all children, including play opportunities that enable exploration and learning from the child's previous experiences.
- Opportunities are afforded to interact with parents and the community to gain a better understanding of the children's contextual experiences and negate any preformed stereotypes.
- Provision of an inclusive environment that enables children and families to have a voice and inform policy and practice.
- Families and community are encouraged to participate in the school at all levels to break down barriers and possible feelings of exclusion.
- A review of staff recruitment procedures and staff development opportunities should be undertaken to ensure diversity within the team.

Each team can interpret the points above according to their own setting, needs and circumstances. Policy decisions should be framed by a commitment to action in recognition of racism as a factor in black children's lives, including their experiences in the early years setting. It is necessary to approach race equality policy with this in mind in order to challenge more covert ways in which children are racialised through everyday procedures and practices. Race equality policies will only address disadvantage through a critique of whiteness and direct action against influences that perpetuate inequalities (Gillborn, 2008). The process of developing race equality policy should be progressive through regular monitoring and discussion with all those involved. It is necessary to allocate staff development time and funding for this purpose to implement critical anti-racist practice that addresses experiences such as those told by the children in this book.

Summary

Individual practitioners or teams may not be able to implement all the actions suggested in this chapter. However, some will be possible or may stimulate other ideas for action towards a more inclusive learning environment. The responsibility of each early years setting to provide appropriately for all children by reviewing and building on good practice is already in place. Settings implement strategies to provide resources and activities that relate to diverse cultures and identities of children and families in Britain as an element of the early years curriculum. All practitioners in this study voice their commitment to providing a safe environment that promotes equality of opportunity for all children across the intersections of race, class, gender and ability. The ideas suggested above are intended to develop that existing good practice towards a critical anti-racist pedagogy to include the more covert practices and processes that create hierarchies of advantage based on racialised identities. The activities aim to introduce discussion and awareness of inherent attitudes that may impact on practice to marginalise black children. They are planned to enable black practitioners and children to voice their own realities regarding racism in an environment where they are listened to and where action will follow. By understanding the subtle and unspoken ways by which young children are racialised through both personal interactions and institutional processes, it is possible to challenge factors that reproduce racism in settings. Each practitioner approaches her or his own personal and professional responsibilities towards an effective anti-racist pedagogy from a starting point of their own life experiences. The ideas in this chapter are intended to support that journey towards an early years education that is different, appropriate and supportive of the lived experience for black children as we hear their stories and challenge their racialisation.

References

Brown, B. (2008) *Equality in Action: A Way Forward with Persona Dolls*. Staffordshire: Trentham Books.

Gillborn, D. (2008) *Racism and Education, Coincidence or Conspiracy*. Oxon: Routledge.

Lane, J. (2008) *Young Children and Racial Justice*. London: National Children's Bureau.

Leonardo, Z. (2009) *Race, Whiteness and Education*. Oxon: Routledge.

MacNaughton, G., Smith, K. and Davis, K. (2007) Researching with Young Children, in Hatch, J. A. (ed.), *Early Childhood Qualitative Research*. Oxon: Routledge.

Rollock, N., et al. (2015) *The Colour of Class*. Oxon: Routledge.

9

CONCLUSION

The children's stories in this study indicate that it is not possible to have equal access to education if the factors impacting on their racialisation are not considered from a young age. Personal stories can frame an early years environment that values and includes the contribution of children's prior cultural knowledge and experiences as integral to everyday practice. They can facilitate support for black children through awareness of stereotypes, interactions and processes in education that can marginalise and discriminate.

A critical early years pedagogy guided through the principles of Critical Race Theory (CRT) (Chapter 1) can support black children to learn and develop within an environment that values their personal identities and cultural contributions. Everyone has a story to tell of how their lives have been influenced by historic and current attitudes to difference within the multiracial arena of British identity. Some stories illustrate the privileges of whiteness, while others relate experiences of personal and structural racism. The revisiting of the Stephen Lawrence murder during the twenty-fifth anniversary of his death is a reminder of the importance of acknowledging the continuing existence of institutionalised racism (BBC, 2018). Denial of racism in British institutions is evident in the accounts of witnesses, family and friends and is familiar to those who experience racism. Through counter-narratives it is possible to understand the impact on society and the need to determine action against the damaging historically embedded stereotypes and social constructs of race. Change can come through a realisation of how whiteness acts, however unintentionally, to discriminate, marginalise and racialise young black children as they form new identities.

The challenges children face have been partly influenced by government decisions regarding a formalised curriculum for the Early Years, where references to cultural diversity are included as an addition to current priorities in content. This has been discussed as resulting in non-critical multiculturalism that excludes rather than includes those British children with generational descent originating from colonisation (Chapter 7). Race has been socially constructed in Britain over centuries of colonisation, slavery and immigration to maintain the hegemony of whiteness (Chapter 1). People from all over the world contribute positively to British culture, although some can view this as a threat to the hierarchy of whiteness and cultural traditionalism. Modern concepts of Britishness are historically evident through immigration since early times: Roman invasion, colonisation, wars bringing refugees and asylum seekers, and European open borders that enable entry for a new workforce and those escaping economic hardship. Attitudes supporting a monocultural, traditionalist Britain exist within a contrary reality manifested by international cuisines that are now integral to the British diet, festivals in which members of all communities participate, music genres enjoyed across the population, languages and dialects that influence spoken English, and social relationships and partnerships. People from the Caribbean arrived in Britain in the 1950s, as British subjects, to rebuild the country after World War Two (Channel 5, 2018). Their families continue to make an immense contribution to all aspects of British society through employment, voluntary work, scientific knowledge, professional expertise, social responsibility, political engagement and the arts. Attitudes transmitted through negative concepts of difference can result in denial of these enriching cultural, social and economic contributions to Britain and Britishness. Communities continue to be othered and disadvantaged by racism, as recently exposed in the media through the denial of British citizenship and rights to those of the Windrush generation and their families from the Caribbean (Channel 4, 2018). Colour-blindness can negate experiences of racism by treating everyone the same as a response to equality. This approach ignores or dismisses the systemic and personal means by which hierarchies of whiteness are unquestionably reinforced to discriminate against others. The experiences of the children in this book cannot be ignored through false premises that equality can be achieved by avoiding the uncomfortable reality of racism as it impacts on young lives. Meaningful communication through ongoing, professionally guided relationships with parents and practitioners across diverse cultural heritages can support social justice in early years education.

The children's stories importantly tell of their resilience to the psychological impact of racialisation as they adjust to new environments. As well as establishing their own strategies, children need support to remain confident to maintain and represent their positive black identities and home cultures. Their friendships are important for this in the transition from home to school, as demonstrated in Devon's story (Chapter 3). Playful pedagogy can enable children to maintain their identities through self-expression while understanding how to adjust to cultural norms of school without compromising their blackness. Play allows for conceptual exploration and understanding from a starting point of cultural familiarity and shared previous knowledge, as in the superhero play of Sonic and his peers (Chapter 4). Playful pedagogy enables children to use their agency to challenge marginalisation by contributing their socio-cultural experiences in pursuit of new knowledge and relationships. Child-centred education is about sharing power between adults and children. However, as demonstrated by Pina (Chapter 5), without intervention and support, play and self-directed activity can reproduce racialised hierarchies and contribute to exclusion. A critical insight into children's play can enable appropriate interventions that encourage children to reflect on their attitudes to difference and provide opportunities for a more egalitarian ethos through which to address racialised norms.

Early years pedagogy centred in the ideology of play and self-directed activity can be framed through CRT by an understanding and acceptance of the many ways race and racism impact on black children's experiences. It provides a theoretical lens to guide anti-racist practice by acknowledging the reality of racism through the counter-stories of those who directly experience the effects. Awareness of racism at institutional and personal levels can inform the development of policy and practice in consideration of the impact on black children's education. Knowledge of how black children are racialised can enable practitioners to give support to them as they resist personal challenges when they occur during everyday interactions. CRT is not only about 'talking the talk' but also requires 'walking the walk' by taking action (Hylton, 2012). Chapter 8 has given suggestions for how action can be taken both individually and in teams. Race equality policy and effective implementation can then operate to walk the walk towards a learning environment that is more inclusive and accessible. Individual early years settings cannot change racist ideology at societal level, as this requires hegemonic change and political commitment to disrupt the permanence of racism (Bell, 2009). However a critical race praxis that recognises racism and challenges the mechanisms of whiteness and racism at a micro level can go some way towards the aim of a socially just education system. Listening to black children's stories can be a starting point for this essential action in early years education.

References

BBC (2018) *Stephen: The Murder That Changed a Nation S01E031.* London: On the Corner/ Rogan Productions for the BBC. Available on UTube. Accessed 2 July 2018.

Bell, D. A. (2009) Brown v. Board of Education and the Interest Convergence Dilemma, in Taylor, E., Gillborn, D. and Ladson-Billings, G. (eds.), *Foundations of Critical Race Theory in Education.* Oxon: Routledge.

Channel 4 News (2018) *Windrush Generation: The Scandal That Shook Britain Explained and Debated.* Available from Utube.com. Accessed 24 April 2018.

Channel 5 (2018) *New: Rivers of Blood 50 Years On.* ITN Productions for Channel 5 Broadcasting Ltd.

Hylton, K. (2012) Talk the Talk, Walk the Walk: Defining Critical Race Theory, in *Race, Ethnicity and Education,* 15 (1) pp. 23–41.

INDEX